doggone

doggone

joe bennett

HAZARD PRESS
publishers

All articles in this book were first published
in the Christchurch *Press*, the *Evening Post*,
the *New Zealand Herald*, *Hawke's Bay Today*
or the *Otago Daily Times*.

For Abes

First published 2002
Copyright © 2002 Joe Bennett

The author asserts his moral rights in the work.

ISBN 1-877270-34-2

Hazard Press is an imprint of Hazard Publishing Limited

Published by Hazard Publishing Limited
P.O. Box 2151, Christchurch, New Zealand
Front cover photograph by John McCombe

Printed in New Zealand

Contents

Foreword 7

I shall 8

The cricket, exclamation mark 10

Cuchulain's children 13

Away with Jane 16

Roosters redundant 18

A call to arms 21

Toast him 24

On her birthday 27

Basta pasta 30

White rectangular domestic things 33

Thread that camel 36

Like solitary sex 39

Living with basil 42

Or else say nothing 45

The end of the soap 48

The good rhinoceros 50

Scatter the dark forces 52

Marconi or someone 55

Permanent, fixed and safe 58

Sliding to happiness 61

Several worsts 64

Sorry, Jim 66

Tom, Dick and Harriet...69

Natch...72

Sallabout...74

Because he is a man...76

A serial preacher..79

Eyes right..81

Going with logs..83

He's in a meeting..86

I wish they didn't...89

Hitchlie..92

Cosh the teacher...94

Déjà drenched..97

Ruling and sucking..100

Down at the elbow...102

Be luggage..105

Gliding through Niceville...108

So mother was right...111

When it rains...114

Gueule de bois..116

Murder your darlings..119

Seven minutes to live...121

Diggers and dozers..124

He was a pretty good dog..126

Foreword

On the desk a bill for a new shower-mixer, an address book open at R, a diary dotted with a cat's pawprints, a stapler, two phones, two ashtrays, three coffee cups, several pens, an advertisement for chewing gum, a kebab skewer I use as a toothpick and an inch-deep slew of papers. I spend much of my time at this desk. The 40-something essays in this book are as near as I get to tidying it.

Under the desk a sleeping dog. Soon I'll take her out to explore the untidy world. She'll love that.

J.B., Lyttelton, 2002

I shall

Yes of course I've made a New Year's resolution. I shall behave better at parties.

When I am going to a party in 2002 I shall not take the bottle of Fijian riesling that someone once brought to my party because someone once brought it to their party. And when I take the Fijian riesling I shall not carry it in with my hand over the label, nor shall I go straight to the kitchen and hide it among the other bottles of Fijian riesling and look in the fridge for beer.

I shall not pretend to recognise people. When someone at a party says, 'Hello Joe, how lovely to see you again', I shall not say it is lovely to see them again. I shall say, 'What's your name?'

When people tell me their name I shall use it five times in the first five sentences so as not to forget it. When I forget it I shall not substitute the word 'mate'.

When I kiss a woman at a party I shall not let the woman dictate how we are going to kiss. I shall decide for myself whether it is to be the lips, the cheek or the full facial bypass. If it is the full facial bypass I shall not nibble the ear. If it is the lips I shall wait a full minute before wiping my mouth. When a man makes to hug me I shall go away.

If a conversation is boring I shall not say that I am just going to fetch a drink and then not come back. I shall say I am just going to the loo and then not come back. If I say I am just going to fetch a drink the bore can ask me to fetch him one too and we are back where we started.

I shall not escape bores by pretending to catch sight of someone I know on the far side of the room and saying, 'Excuse me a minute.' Nor shall I beckon a friend across, introduce the friend to the bore and then go away.

If a friend beckons me across to meet someone I shall go away. I shall go to the back doorstep to smoke and play with the dog.

I shall not spend long periods at parties sitting on the back doorstep smoking and playing with the dog. Nor shall I steal chicken vol-au-vents to feed the dog with. Nor shall I give it sips of Fijian riesling.

I shall always take a warm sweater to parties because it can get cold on the back door step. A cushion would be a good idea too. And some chicken vol-au-vents.

When the party begins at 8 o'clock I shall not go to the pub first for just a quick one. Nor shall I stay at home with a book until it is too late to go to the party and then ring up in the morning and say I've just looked in the diary and how sorry I am to have missed it and was it fun and we must do it again soon.

I shall never say we must do it again soon.

When someone at a party tells me something private and juicy I shall not tell it to the next person I talk to without first asking them if they can keep a secret. If they say no I shall not just go ahead and tell them anyway.

When people ask me if I can keep a secret I shall say no. They will just go ahead and tell me anyway.

I shall not stay right to the end of parties. When I stay right to the end of parties I shall not boast that I used to be reasonably good at gymnastics. When I boast that I used to be reasonably good at gymnastics I shall not offer to do a handstand. I shall always choose a well-carpeted bit of the house to do the handstand in.

When people at parties ask me if I'd be willing to help out with the bring-and-buy sale for the local kindergarten I shall say no. And when they ring up the next day to ask if I really meant it when I said yes, I shall not say, 'Of course I meant it.' I shall say, 'No, I didn't mean it.'

When they tell me the date of the bring-and-buy sale I shall not say, 'What a pity. I'll be out of town that day.' Nor shall I then go out of town that day in case someone rings from the bring-and-buy sale.

When the beer runs out at parties I shall not drink from left-over cans that are half full. I shall sieve them first to get the cigarette ends out.

I shall not dance.

The cricket, exclamation mark

S orry but no,' I said into the receiver. 'It's kind of you and I'd really like to go. I just love Bulgarian films, especially from the 50s, those gritty black and white tonal values, that daring absence of plot, but it's just...'

'You want to watch the cricket,' she said.

'The cricket,' I said with vehemence, 'the cricket, exclamation mark. Yes I do.'

'Cricket,' she said in the manner of a public health official diagnosing threadwarts, 'is 20 boys who somehow got through puberty but didn't let it change a thing, wasting five days of what they like to think of as their lives playing a game devised in the 19th century to keep schoolboys from masturbating and the British Empire from revolting, a game that, if it ever had any virtue, has now surrendered it entirely to commercial interests.'

'Twenty-two boys,' I said.

'Haven't you noticed,' she swept on, 'that the team from this country is sponsored by an offshore telecommunications company and that the team from the other country is sponsored by another offshore telecommunications company and that the whole shebang is televised by a third offshore telecommunications company whose only purpose is to keep drongos like you rooted to the sofa, beer in hand and brain in neutral, cramming pepperoni pizzas into your mouth for 50 years until you die? You're a dupe, a stooge, a dummy, a victim of commercial manipulation, a life-form in suspension, a passive receptacle for trash, a donkey at the water wheel drawn ever forward by the synthetic allure of the business of sport. It's manhood by proxy, war by proxy, nationalism by proxy.' She paused for breath.

'I wish,' I said, 'you wouldn't say offshore. What's wrong with foreign? Or,' I added conciliatorily, 'even overseas', but she was in no mood for conciliation.

'The saddest thing of all,' she said, and the word 'said' comes nowhere near accommodating the rising swell of her passion, 'are the people known as commentators, aged fools who once upon a time were young and played the game until their bodies betrayed them and who were then so deeply terrified of having to grow up that they scuttled like so many shell-less hermit crabs into the commentary box where they could bathe forever in the perpetual infancy of reminiscence and mendacity.'

'I see,' I said.

'Is that all,' she snorted, 'all you've got to say to defend the way you choose to spend a day of your life?'

'It ought to be,' I said, 'but since you ask, it isn't. Cricket's beautiful.'

Her gasp was gratifying.

'Truly beautiful,' I said. 'Like you,' I almost added, before wisdom stilled my tongue. 'Have you not,' I asked, 'seen Shane Warne? A man whose manner I find utterly repellent, a man who has the aura of a moral vacuum, a man whom I would cross the road to miss, but a man who bowls a cricket ball as Leonardo wielded paint. To watch him shuffle with his surfboy hair a few short strides towards the stumps, his wrist furled up, his fingers wrapped like tentacles around the ball and then to toss a leg break up in such a way that it will dip and curve and land and bite and spit and leave a batsman baffled, that, my dear, is beauty. Forget the artist – Leonardo, after all, had pimples and breath like Agent Orange – but love the art.

'And have you not,' I added, 'seen Stephen Fleming bat? He gropes and looks ungainly and then from furnaces where art is forged he leans onto a bent front knee and puts the ball past extra cover so sweetly that confectioners swoon. The right elbow may not be elevated as the coaching books would wish but that's the imperfection that makes beauty. There are moments when he conjures up a hint of David Gower, and praise can go no higher. Gower batted like the Holy Ghost in whites.

'I could go on,' I said. 'I could tell you of a dumpy little Englishman called Philip Sharpe who caught the ball at slip with such deft ease I swear that, had he wished, he could have plucked a swallow from the summer air.

'And even,' I continued, 'in these grim commercial times of sponsorship and chewing gum, the sport can still produce a game like the one that has just been, a game that over five long days swung one way then the other, a game embracing luck and misery along the way, and heroism, courage, subtlety and thought, a game of such intensity it drained the colour from my hair. And in the end it was a draw. Beat that for irony,' I said. 'Beat that for simulation of the way we are. Beat that.'

She couldn't. She'd gone.

Cuchulain's children

No, no, it just won't do, this Irish stuff. It's got to stop. Now I'm as fond of a pint of stout as the next man, so come St Patrick's Day the next man and I duly toddled down to the joke local Irish bar where the heirs to the warrior tradition of Cuchulain the Strong were wearing wigs of green tinsel. But at least they'd maintained the ancient Irish tradition of emigrating.

So many Paddies have hightailed it out of Ireland that only the Catholic church's sexual ethics have kept the place populated. Not that there's anything wrong with emigrating. I've done a fair swag of it myself but if you ever catch me boohooing for the land of my birth, kindly take a shillelagh to my softer parts then lash me to the mizzen of the first ship home.

The Irish have made boohooing into an art. Apart from people, their only export crop is nostalgia, as summed up by the character in a Hardy novel who 'sang sweet songs of his own dear country that he loved so much as never to have revisited it'. Because, of course, no sooner is Paddy O'Flaherty on the boat bound for Opportunity than he's humming 'Danny Boy', going misty-eyed at any mention of the Emerald Isle and acquiring a rackful of CDs by Daniel O'Bleeding Donnell.

Most of the Irish have emigrated for that most cogent of reasons, poverty. Too few spuds on the table for a family of 27 meant Liam took the first boat to New York where his love of fighting after the pub shut would lead him naturally into the police force. Once there he could start lying.

Liam and his mates the world over have woven not so much a tissue of lies about poor old Ireland as a heavy-duty tarpaulin. And it's a tarpaulin that the rest of the world, in the manner of a snake ingesting a goat, has swallowed.

Bung the word Irish in front of anything these days and it sells. Irish ballads, Irish tenors, and, most wonderful of all, traditional Irish dancing featuring a man in traditional sequined trousers and a line up of colleens in apt but invisible straitjackets, all of them heel-and-toeing it as if picking their way through an IRA bomb stash. The whole shebang is as authentically Irish as coq au vin.

Heritage, they call it, of a piece with the rich Irish literary tradition starring Jonathan Swift who spent three-quarters of his life in London, James Joyce who set up shop in either Paris or Zurich – I can't remember and don't care which, and neither did he, so long as it wasn't Dublin – and dreary Sam Beckett who did most of his waiting for O'Godot on the left bank of the Seine. Most recently we've had Frank McCourt. Son of a stout-sodden ne'er-do-well who spectacularly failed to keep his family of 50 in bread and pigsheads, dear old Frank headed across the Atlantic with understandable haste to write an account of his childhood with such lyrical intensity that every author envies him his deprivation. His tumbledown place of birth has become a shrine for semi-literate female tourists who've fallen in love with the heaving of Michael Flatley's chest or Val Doonican's cable-knit cardigan.

And then there are the Irish pubs. Oh spare us. To qualify as an Irish pub you've got to serve Guinness and play an over-loud CD of fiddle music. That's it. Plus a dozen green balloons on March 17th and a sturdy bag for lugging the loot to the bank. Irish pubs have sprung up wherever market research has revealed an untapped seam of bogus sentiment. That means everywhere. A former pupil of mine who's as Irish as a mob of hoggets has recently opened one in Sao Paulo. Hong Kong's got them like measles. The only place that hasn't got Irish pubs as the world knows them is Ireland.

I've been to Ireland. It's wet. The typical pub holds a wall-eyed son of the soil called Pete gobbing gloomily into a fire of the same name and wondering why he didn't join Dominic, Moirag et al on the first boat to Elsewhere, while the raddled barmaid breaks occasionally into a basso profundo rendition of 'One Day at a Time, Sweet Jesus' in the hope of sucking in a tourist. Meanwhile round the back of this scene of Irish authenticity lurks a bulldozer with the engine running on Euro tax dollars just waiting for the nod from Brussels to bowl the wreck of a pub and put up a tilt slab factory to assemble a thousand televisions a day so the tourist board can continue to beam images of old Ireland to every expatriate Paddy in the globe.

If you imagine we live in a secular age, freed from the superstitious burden of myth, just think Ireland.

Away with Jane

A m urban man. Pampered, pale and unable to read a compass, I prefer books to bush. If I want to get in touch with nature I wind the car window down.

What little I do know of the natural world I learned from outdoor education. In the unlovely jargon of teaching, outdoor education is a rarity because it means precisely what it says. It happens outdoors and it educates. Or at any rate it educated me.

In 20 years of teaching I learned that before being allowed to go on a school camp teachers had to meet a set of rigorous criteria. They had to have four limbs, be under 100 years old, and be slower than their colleagues at thinking up ways to get out of it. I met all criteria. Thus once a year I would find myself dumped in a place I didn't want to be in, with 50 children I didn't want to be with. I would know I was a week away from a warm shower and a set of thermal underwear away from frostbite. It taught me a lot. It taught me, as it taught King Lear, that 'the art of our necessities is strange, and can make vile things precious'.

The art of our necessities means distinguishing fripperies from essentials. In the great outdoors fripperies are clean underpants. Essentials, on the other hand, are wire coat-hangers and a novel by Jane Austen.

In the bush Jane Austen kept me sane. Every night when the day's horrors were done and the kids had finally retired to their wet tents and lay together grumbling with excitement and I realised with relief that I was 24 hours closer to an innerspring mattress, I would check the ridge of my tent, murder the mosquitoes that dangled there, then get into bed with Miss Austen. With a rucksack beneath my head and a torch beneath my chin and Jane Austen on my chest I would withdraw into the early 19th century where delight was a handsome curate and horror a twisted ankle. And as the rain beat its little hammers on the canvas and the creatures of the night made moan, Jane Austen made me happy.

So did the coat-hangers. A coat-hanger can be broken into lengths, bent into shapes and used to mend a thousand things. But above all it is metal. Break off a length of 6 inches or so, bend it into an S and you have a billy hook. You can suspend your billy directly over the camp fire and you can make coffee. Coffee is not a frippery.

The children envied me my billy hooks. Their envy taught them economics. They would try to buy the billy hooks with money. But in the bush money is good only for starting fires. They would offer me food. I had enough food. One boy once offered me his Walkman. He could not make hot drinks with his Walkman. If nothing else he learned that value is a variable.

The one essential I could not carry with me into the bush was plumbing. Each trip I rediscovered the discomfort of what I had better call alfresco evacuation. It took me years to learn how to beat the problem.

What I learned was to hold a dunny-building competition. I would challenge the groups of children to create in two hours a dunny with every possible luxury to it. The prize would be chocolate. The children would do anything for chocolate. They improvised brilliantly. They made dunnies with moulded seats of rock . They made foot-rests, back-rests, roll-holders, even book-holders. They made thatched roofs and little gates for privacy. I would inspect their creations and award the prizes. And then I would take the winners to one side and I would cut a deal. I would buy the best dunny for my exclusive use. The price of this real estate would be 6 inches of coat-hanger.

But of all the mornings of outdoor education I remember one with clarity. It had rained for three days. Gloom had curled its arms about us all. The tents were sodden. The Weetbix were sodden. Even Jane Austen was sodden. She had turned translucent and her pages had to be peeled apart. And then I woke at dawn to the fish tank effect of sun through canvas. I unzipped my tent and emerged into a world that steamed.

I felt my limbs unfurl and my dank flesh drink at the warmth. I sat on a rock overlooking the quilt of the Canterbury Plains and for once I saw the sun for what it is. I felt outdoors and educated. Beside me Jane Austen dried and crinkled.

Roosters redundant

My two roosters crow and fight and preen and strut and mount their mothers. My roosters are beautiful and useless. No one wants them. In their uselessness they tell the story of tomorrow – the future is female.

On any farm most male animals are slaughtered young. Roosters are macerated by a machine that should be called Herod. At present we have no Herod for the human species, but neither shall we need one. The engineers who will put paid to the human male will be the genetic boffins. Boys and men are doomed.

Genetic engineering has broken all the fences. It is now careering across unmapped territory. The future is easy to imagine but hard to swallow.

The boffins could already clone people. They could engineer an infinite sequence of nice girls who would not crow or fight or strut or preen or bicker. And it is inevitable that they will.

The fate of males is evident in my roosters. I should have killed and eaten them but I have a girly heart. I advertised them. Two people rang. The first was a man who has acquired a rooster to use as an alarm clock, but isn't happy with it. Apparently it says the cockadoodle but omits the do. He asked if my roosters did the do. I said that yes, they did the do. He said he would take the prettier one – a golden Wyandotte.

The second call came from a woman who has a few acres. At the far end of her paddocks lives a colony of roosters. The neighbouring farmer used to keep chooks and he let nature take its course which meant that his roosters fought for supremacy. Those that lost had to pack their bags. They took refuge in a distant stand of macrocarpas where they now live together in peace because they have no hens to fight over nor purpose to live for. They peck for grubs and seeds and huddle in the branches at night bragging about the past, watching television and listlessly discussing rugby. And that, boys, will be us. There will be no need for us. We will have scienced ourselves out of a job.

Men are redundant. A few may be kept on in guarded reservations to be milked for sperm to keep the gene pool fresh and bubbly, but with cloning there will be no need even for that.

A few other specimens may be bred and kept to do manual labour. But we will be sterilised and supervised and locked up at night. And we shall have no cause to complain. We screwed up. We fought and shouted and trod on each other. The women told us to grow up but we did not listen because we had muscles. If we could find no one to fight we drank beer and bought war videos and played snooker. We've been out to grass for years but we never noticed.

Time was when we did everything. We did the science and wrote the books and ran the businesses and made the money and farmed the animals and played the sport. Women, we said, could do none of these things. We were wrong. The 20th century has proved us wrong. And in proving us wrong it also proved us to be useless except as donors of sperm. And now the 21st century is ready to remove that sole remaining purpose. Our extinction makes clear rational sense.

We evolved to fight in the endless war of evolution. That war is over. Killing will stop when we stop. Crime will stop when we stop.

The neat irony of this is that we men also built religions. It is as if we knew we were bad. The most durable of those religions extol qualities like tolerance and peace and harmony and loving our neighbours and sacrificing ourselves for others. These are not the things we do. These are things women do.

We pictured a heaven where the good things happened. We called it utopia which means nowhere. We did not believe that heaven could be made on earth, but it can and it will. The women will make it. It must happen. It is called progress and as we have been telling women for centuries, nothing can stand in the way of progress.

The women of heaven will not seek to grow rich at the expense of others. They will care. They will live on solar power and recycled yoghurt. The world will turn green again and the football paddocks will be planted in soya. Fish will swim, birds will fly. Only gentle things will happen. Endlessly. It will be bloody boring. Cockadoodle do.

A call to arms

Whoa! Rein the horses, stop the wagon train, form a circle, shelter the women and children, load the muskets and prepare to do battle. (On second thoughts, just shelter the children: the women of today are up to it.) The vandals have come down from the hills and civilisation is under threat. (On third thoughts might as well let the children have a go too. If they can put up with body piercing they can go to war. If anyone needs shelter today it's the men.) But it's time to kill or be killed. If we lose this one, well, who cares? It will be all over and there will be nothing left to fight for. Sound the bugle, sing heigh ho, for this is it, the big one, the decisive engagement between culture and barbarism, and there's something scary but pleasing after decades of decline to have the enemy in plain view. Now at last we have something to shoot at. The years of endurance are over and courtesy is long gone. These are raw days. The enemy has a name and a form at last. It is called the Bee Gees.

You've heard the story. Students of English at the University of Cambridge sit a compulsory paper on the subject of tragedy. That tragedy is the only compulsory paper deserves an article on its own with a fat dose of irony, but now is no time for irony. Now is the time for cold steel.

Those who set this exam have stooped to baseness. After years of blameless academic purity – 'Ibsen's tragic vision was predicated on the image of disease. Discuss'; 'Address the notion of literal and metaphorical blindness in the tragic oeuvre' etc – they have let down their guard and the subculture of inanity has thrown a right hook through the gap. That right hook is the Bee Gees.

The walls of academe have crumbled, eaten out by the maggot called relevance. And that maggot has crawled onto the exam paper in the form of the following words:

Tragedy
When the feeling's gone and you can't go on
It's tragedy
When you lose control and you've got no soul
It's tragedy.

Words written by the Bee Gees. It is tempting at this point simply to take sides, to throw in one's lot with the Mounted Battalion of the Educated Few and rally beneath a standard on which is embroidered the legend, 'We shall not dumb down'. The Bee Gees represent everything that education is supposed to drag us out of. They are a pop group – nasty – they are impossibly wealthy – nastier still – and they cause men and women of unimaginable poverty of mind to form 'fan clubs', groups of such unmitigated awfulness that we must needs be protected from the possibility of infection by shrouding them in inverted commas.

But though the temptation is strong, it ignores the fact that the Bee Gees' words make a rather good question. They invite debate and disagreement and that is what exam questions are for. Consider Macbeth – by Act V (oh, that lovely educated V) he has lost the power to feel the virtuous emotions of pity or grief – has lost, in short, his soul – and can go on only as a murderous automaton. That indeed, as the Bee Gees suggest, is tragedy. Meanwhile Mrs Macbeth has lost control and cannot go on in any way at all. She flings herself from the battlements. That too is tragedy.

Ah ha, perhaps so, scream the defenders of the faith, but the Bee Gees didn't know that. They just flung a few emotive words together, found that they rhymed and sang them. And besides, the masses who writhe and squirm to their 'music' (more disinfectant punctuation) pay no attention to the lyrics of the songs. Those lyrics are merely noise, an anodyne addition to the simian rhythm of the drums and that crudest of instruments, the electric guitar. The Bee Gees know not what they say. They gibber like parrots, but are incapable of consecutive thought.

Well, perhaps so and perhaps not. Nevertheless I think we should note the fundamental irony in all this. The great tragedians, whose work we revere but don't read, were the Bee

Gees of their day. Look at the size of the theatres in Athens. Four-fifths of the population rolled up to see Aeschylus's latest blood-spattered epic. Or consider the impoverished groundlings at Shakespeare's Globe with their bad breath and worse armpits. The ancient tragedians were popular. Popular does not mean bad.

But I argue against myself. I have been trained in cultural supremacy. My education obliges me to take arms against a sea of Bee Gees. Don't shoot till you can see the whites of their teeth.

Toast him

If you were planning to do great things, things that would rock the earth's foundations and make you *Time* magazine's person of the year, forget it. Postpone your plans till 2003 because 2002 is spoken for. I have no doubt that the front cover of the December issue of *Time* has already been put to bed. Come Christmas we'll be raising our glasses to big Brian Savill.

Actually he may not be big. From the newspaper story I have read I know only that Brian Savill is 47 years old. He may, for all I know, be weedy, bald and paunchy, with spectacles, erectile problems and an unreliable Ford Escort, but none of that matters a jot. Just as Snell had his mile, Hillary his Everest, and Newton and Adam their apples, so in 2002 Brian Savill has had his moment of apotheosis.

The setting for this apotheosis was as mundane as they come: a sodden soccer pitch in Eastern England and a game of no account. The wind swept off the gaunt North Sea. Of the spectators, one left early because he was frozen to the bone and the other stayed only to bark at seagulls.

The game was not a close one. With ten minutes left the score stood at Earls Colne 18, Wimple 1. The teeth of the Earls Colne goalkeeper were chattering like a typewriter. Even the Earls Colne strikers had tired of the massacre. Only one of their number, a shaven-headed weasel, kept them at it, urging them to score an unprecedented 20 goals.

Then a miracle occurred. Somehow the ball found its way to the Earls Colne end. It bounced off a fullback's knee, bypassed the hypothermic keeper and lodged in the mud in front of an open goal. And it was at toast moment that Brian Savill stepped up and casually booted it into the net: 18–2. For a moment all was silence. Both teams stood like statues. Even the wind abated as Brian Savill, with spectacular nonchalance, raised his hand to his mouth and blew his whistle. 'Goal,' he said. For Brian Savill was the referee.

The shaven-headed one ran straight at Brian. He put his face an inch or two from Brian's and he said words. Brian Savill turned away. The goal stood.

Brian Savill's been a referee for eighteen years. He likes his sport. But in that fraction of a second when the ball appeared in front of him he heard a voice. It rose from a great depth, a depth that normally is plugged and silent. It rose from a deep seam of mischief. It rose from a sense of the ridiculous. It rose like a giggle and Mr Savill, bless his little referee's shorts, gave in to it.

What Mr Savill committed was an act of comedy. Comedy's anarchic. It's founded in surprise, surprise that pulls the rug from under the feet of the serious and sends them toppling. And that's exactly what the shaven-headed weasel couldn't stand.

Inevitably someone ratted on Brian Savill. And so last week the Essex County Football Association Disciplinary Committee summoned him to appear before them and with the power vested in them by the national football association they sentenced him to a seven-week suspension.

In the same week as Scottish football fans threw sharpened coins, invaded a pitch and fought, the good committee men of Essex found Mr Savill guilty of bringing the game into disrepute. In the same week as an American was found guilty of beating his son's hockey coach to death, they condemned Mr Savill for inappropriate behaviour on a sporting field. In the same week as I heard a man on talkback radio boast that he had taught his cricketing son never to walk when he knew he was out and to take every chance to sledge the opposition, they judged Mr Savill to be a bad sport.

Of course Mr Savill was guilty, but not as charged. The crime the mandarins could not forgive was that Mr Savill had said sport is sport and in the end it doesn't matter as much as all that. He'd done something funny.

Comedy is serious. It cocks a snook. Mr Savill cocked a snook at all the shaven-headed weasels of this world. He cocked a snook at dull committee men, at self-importance, at the talkback ranters and the sledgers and the Yours Disgusteds. He showed, quite simply, a sense of proportion.

Angels can fly, said Chesterton, because they take themselves lightly. For one brief moment Brian Savill, my man of the year 2002, flew with them.

On her birthday

Rumours have gone about and I intend to scotch them. They vary in detail but they all feature a character answering my own description wandering the streets in a state of undress on the morning of Her Majesty's official birthday.

I care little for my own reputation but it galls me to think that others may think that the Queen has lost one of her stoutest supporters – though I can't say stout would be my adjective of choice. My mother's term was big-boned.

Anyway, call me a throwback, call me an anachronism, but I'm a monarchist. Was it not I that traipsed down to the harbour in Victoria, British Columbia some 20 years ago to stand at the back of a vast crowd to catch a glimpse of Her Majesty's hat? Indeed so. The hat was purple.

So last Sunday on the eve of the Queen's official birthday I retired early to my humble three-poster – the fourth poster, an intimate snap of Her Majesty strangling a pheasant, fell from the wall some months ago. The cat got to it. I miss it still.

I divested myself slowly of my formal daywear, replacing it with a pair of Cashmere pyjamas, Merivale bedsocks, and a Fendalton nightcap that has aroused envy among the fashion-conscious. Suburban nightwear perhaps, but Christchurch suburban at least.

Folding back the hand-crocheted counterpane, I extracted a dried pea, a paper-clip and something yellow from between the inviting sheets, lay down, scanned a few pages of *The Bumper Bedside Picture Book of the House of Windsor* (with its illustrated appendix on Romanian bloodlines) and turned out the light. I spent my last waking moments imagining just what the mighty Empress of the Falklands herself might be doing at that moment.

With cheeky affection I pictured her sneaking down the palace stairs in the middle of the night, alone but for a guttering candle and a brace of ladies of the bedchamber, to peek at the pile of tributes laid out for her inspection in the morning. The eviction notice from nice Mr Blair, the trouser-suit catalogue from our own prime minister, and the large intriguing parcel that rattled when she shook it and which she desperately hoped would prove, when the wrapping came off, to be a little bit of Africa. How she must miss Africa. When she ascended the throne half a century ago most of Africa came attached.

Popular music woke me. My neighbour's a republican. He was holding a party, celebrating not having to get up the next morning by not going to bed that night. The ceaseless beat of his celebrations rumbled down the piles of his house, through our adjoining gardens and up my own piles in a manner that would have delighted Mr Richter.

Sleep was impossible. I tried thinking the sweetest royal thoughts – croquet, polo on corgiback, dubbing a big-boned knight of the realm – but it was no good. I rose and poured myself a soporific of three parts scotch to one part whisky. In deference to the royal anniversary, I diluted it with a dash of malt. The anthropoidal music thundered on. Into the small hours it thundered, and then into the medium-sized ones.

I decided to act. Firm was my stride as I ascended the hill, fierce my expression as I turned through the neighbour's shabby gate, emphatic my finger as I advanced on the bell push, huge my surprise as the door opened even before I could ring.

'Darling!' exclaimed a woman. Ignoring my remonstrations, she swept me into the throng. Grins on every side, composed of one part guilt at their excess and three parts admiration of my get-up. Fingers whisked my nightcap from my head within seconds and passed it from guest to guest with a reverential tossing motion. I fretted for its vulnerable viscose.

A fruit punch was thrust into my hand. Invited to dance I strove to introduce some suitably formal ballroom quality to the thrashing chaos. It proved popular. It also proved warm work. My pyjama top went AWOL. Only a strong sense of decorum prevented the trousers from following it.

To shorten a long and sorry tale, the fruit punch proved Trojan. I woke at nine on the neighbour's sofa amid a scene by Hieronymus Bosch. Strewn bodies, bottles, ashtrays and detumescent balloons. It was the Queen's birthday. The grim leopard of guilt sank its claws instantly into my skull. There was no time to search for missing garments.

That I turned left out of the gate instead of right I ascribe to sheer panic. I met no one on the streets but enough net curtains twitched at my passing for me to know that the rumour mill would grind. And ground it has. I have laid the facts at your feet. Judge me as you will.

Basta pasta

The only time I've been to Italy I got stuck in a town called, if I remember rightly, Soporifico. I'd been told it was a good place to hitch from.

I stood beside the road in Soporifico for four hours. Just before dusk an ox-cart went by. I stuck my thumb out. The ox didn't stop. I was marooned in Soporifico for the night.

Dinner in Soporifico's only restaurant was my first encounter with authentic Italian cuisine. The meal comprised a large plate of pasta followed by a vast plate of pasta. This was complemented by a side dish of pasta. I got halfway through the first plate before rolling quietly off my chair, across the floor of the restaurant and into the road to explode. Some of my fellow diners laughed. The others squabbled over my leftovers.

As a child I knew nothing of pasta. I knew only spaghetti. It came in a tin and was popular with mothers because it was cheap, and with children because it tasted of tomato sauce. It was also fun to throw.

At university spaghetti was still fun to throw – as P.J. O'Rourke has observed, it's cooked when it sticks to the wall – but I now bought it in the form of frail brown sticks. And I learned that the word spaghetti derived from 'spago' meaning 'string', and 'hetti' meaning 'too long to fit into any known saucepan'. It invariably formed the fundament of a dish called Bolognaise. I have not been to Bologna but I presume it is a brownish-red puddle of a city with lumps.

Spaghetti can just about be eaten with cutlery, but not with dignity. However you twirl it there remains a tail. When you suck the tail down it slaps you round the cheeks like a midwife.

Then suddenly, some fifteen years ago, spaghetti became respectable. It shook off its plastic supermarket wrapper, slid into an tall glass jar with a cork stopper, and became an indispensable ingredient in magazine photographs of posh kitchens. At the same time it changed its name to pasta.

In the process it acquired a whole family of relatives named after Italian motorbikes. Vermicelli, tagliatelle, fettuccine – the pretentious rolled the words around their mouths to taste the foreign sophistication. But however much they rolled the stuff itself around their mouths it tasted like spaghetti. Because all pasta, regardless of shape, tastes of nothing. Pasta is bulk food.

Primitive man discovered he could make bulk food out of grain. It was dreary stuff, serving only to supply the energy for going out and hunting a main course. Every part of the world developed its own bulk food.

Northern Europe grew wheat and made bread. The Scots grew oats and made porridge. Some bits of Asia grew rice and made rice, while other bits of Asia grew plants of the genus styrofomus and made noodles.

The English grew barley and made beer. Beer didn't help the English in their hunting but it did stop them worrying about it. Meanwhile the Italians devised a method of removing the flavour from wheat and drying the remains. They called it pasta.

And several thousand years later pasta has come into vogue. In some ways it is easy to see why. The modern world wants speed and convenience. Pasta takes less time to boil than potatoes and doesn't have to be peeled.

And pasta sauces are simple too. Some are tomato-based. These are red and they have exotic names. They taste of tomato. The rest are cream-based. They taste of cream.

At heart pasta is dull stuff – simple, filling and monotonous. Yet it's become a cult. Supermarket shelves are crammed with a thousand indistinguishable brands of pasta sauce. Cookery shops are stacked to the gunwales with pasta machines and pasta strainers and dinky little tools with teeth on them for picking pasta up and putting it down again. I cannot tell you why. Nor can I explain why those appalling busybodies who tell me what I should and shouldn't eat are so in favour of pasta. Italians are just as fat as we are. Nor yet, while I'm at it, can I tell you why our television screens are awash with moustached Italian papas, implausibly large families and ancient crones in sepia who toothlessly sing the praises of some synthetic spread that once brushed by an olive tree.

All I can tell you is that I left Soporifico the following morning by the first available ox.

White rectangular domestic things

Glory be to God for dappled things, said Gerard Manley Hopkins, going on to sing a hymn of praise to feathers on a thrush's chest and speckles on a trout. And that's just fine by me. I like those things a lot, or quite a lot, or somewhat anyway. But though I'm happy for the thrush and trout, as far as I'm concerned it's glory be to God for white rectangular domestic things. You know the things I mean, the tomb-like metal boxes coated in enamel by a process I can only guess at, the boxes that stand mute and patient round the house, the things we notice only when they go kaput and then because they very rarely do. I mean the washing machine. I mean the stove and tumble drier, and, most glorious of all the glories owing unto Him on high, the fridge. They also serve who only stand and hum.

The fridge is loyal and steadfast as a dog that doesn't need to go for walks – although admittedly in one of Owen Marshall's lovely stories there's a fridge that wanders through a farmhouse kitchen, driven by its lurching motor, cubical and android and tethered by a leash of brown electric cable, but even then it's not a threat to flesh, just idiosyncratically quaint.

My own fridge never wanders. For fifteen years I've fed it with a tiny quantity of lifeblood from the national grid and in exchange it's kept its faith with me. It may have come, I don't recall, with densely worded guarantees protecting me from shoddy workmanship, but if it did that guarantee has long since disappeared and rotted in some unremembered place, and all the while the fridge has chuntered on, a self-containing cube of chilliness, a geographic region in itself, distinct and unaffected by the vagaries of weather in the world beyond. Somehow, unlike the other stuff about the house, it doesn't seem to gather dirt. For though I never run a cleaning cloth about its walls, it stands amid the squalor like a virgin in a brothel.

For sure appalling crud collects beneath it, stuff that's greasy brown and sticky, stuff that takes a day of scrubbing with a brush to shift – or 30 seconds licking from a dog – but to blame the fridge for that would be to lay the blame on Downing Street for sheltering Tony Blair.

It's got no catch upon its door. I don't know how it does it but it opens with the application of a feather touch and it closes with a gentleness that couldn't hurt the fingers of the frailest child, and yet when closed it's sealed as surely as a sleeping eye. Not even that most daring of adventurers, the ant, can pierce the fridge's seal. The ant that undissuadably infests all places that it shouldn't, the ant whose six incessant legs will one day tread the earth in meek supremacy, the ant that feasts on scraps and dust and eyes of corpses, the ant that seeps through cracks as thin as hairs, the ant that dies unmourned in millions devoted to its species' greater good, the ant that can move boulders from its path and men to tears, can't penetrate my fridge's silent gentle seal.

A fridge is testament to men. By men I don't mean man in general, I mean men, specific men with names and families, men who over the long centuries have fathomed how to wrest a metal out of rock, who've somehow found the way to manufacture plastic, who've buried taps in trees and sauntered from the forest with a cup of rubber, who've harnessed electricity from lakes, who've played with brains and fingers to construct a motor that just goes on going on.

Yet I, though born and raised in the most technical of centuries, am capable of none of these extraordinary things. I take them as my due for being me. I sip the sweat that poured from others' brows and never give my deep dependency a second thought, reserving for myself the right to pout and sulk and squeal that I'm hard done by, that I fall upon the thorns of life and bleed, without acknowledging that I am blessed with ease and plenty and a fridge.

Why, even 50 years ago a fridge was rare as honesty. In those days milk went off and butter melted, a fish in summer lasted only hours and salmonella flourished. If summer food was to be tasted in the winter it had to be preserved and rendered sour with vinegar or salt, or boiled or pickled, dried or cured or sealed in great preserving jars like surgeon's specimens. Those ancient arts no longer matter much. The fridge has done them down.

So Gerard Manley Hopkins, Jesuit and poet, glory be to God for thrush and trout indeed, but I beg leave to add the fridge is cool.

Thread that camel

You're a bishop. You're heading home after a hard day's bishoping. You trudge through the snow towards your sixteen-room, three-million-dollar official residence. At your approach, a lackey opens the door. A rhomboid of warmth and light slants out across the snow. You smell rich cooking.

The lackey divests you of your robe and mitre, hangs your crook in the cupboard under the ballroom stairs, anoints your feet with goosedown slippers and leads you to the library where a fire blazes. He draws a deep armchair in front of the fire, lowers you gently into it, places a glass of something bracing in your pudgy hand and withdraws to grill you a carp. You sigh. You gaze at the flames and sink into reverie.

There's a knock at the door. The lackey fails to hear it because of the screams of the carp he is at that moment disembowelling.

'Come in,' you bellow.

Nothing.

You sigh with irritation, haul your belly from the chair and slipper your way to the door. You open it.

Nothing. Only the long gleam of the snow. You make to close the door.

'Excuse me.' The voice is thin, weedy, but assertive. It comes from below. You look down. A worm is sidling over the threshold.

'Sorry to intrude, Bish,' says the worm, 'but I'm your conscience. Mind if I come in?'

What to do? Well, that's an easy one. With a single movement of a goosedown slipper you grind the worm into the shag-pile, slam the door and return as swiftly as your bulk permits to the armchair, pausing only to refill your glass from the decanter and to toss another heretic on the fire.

Unless, that is, you are Father Patrick O'Donoghue. Father O'Donoghue, the Roman Catholic Bishop of Lancaster, bless his purple soutane, opened the door to the worm of conscience. He let it in and heard it out.

And the worm told him to hit the road. 'Sell your sixteen-room official residence,' said the worm, 'buy yourself a pair of tramping boots, give the rest of the dosh to charity and hit the road.'

And that is exactly what the bish plans to do. 'We need a revolution in the church,' he announced to the press. 'I want to become a bishop on the move.' His words have thrown a shudder through the establishment.

For Father O'Donoghue has gone back to first principles. He has gone back to the principles of the man who founded his church. Even a knowledge of the Bible as skeletal as mine suggests that he who overturned the tables of the moneychangers, who preached that the meek shall inherit the earth, who mortified his own flesh, who put his trust in powers above to deliver what he needed, who compared a rich man's chances of getting to heaven to a seamstress's chances of threading a camel, would not have approved of sixteen-room residences for his disciples.

Father O'Donoghue's revolution may fail. In the end all revolutions do. The wheel comes round full circle and often, as the dreary but clear-sighted Orwell never tired of pointing out, the revolution spawns a system as bad as, or worse than, the one it overthrew. The French revolution led eventually to the guillotine, the Russian revolution to the KGB and the original Christian revolution to the Vatican owning a bank.

Revolutions mimic the passage of time. The furnace of youth and the grand plans to change the world shrink to the cold ashes of pragmatism and a pension plan.

Father O'Donoghue's revolution may fail swiftly. He'll be a quaint figure, an eccentric, one to be tolerated for a year or two, a minor celebrity followed for a while by a television crew. Then when the fuss dies down, the ecclesiastical authorities, secure once more in their structure, will nudge him quietly out of office and install a less threatening bishop.

On the other hand, the revolution may prove popular for a while. I hope it does. I like the idea of our roads awash with mendicant bishops, shambling bearded figures in inadequate purple rags, knocking on doors to beg a twist of tea, reminding all the frantic go-ahead populace that there is more to life than an inner-sprung mattress and a holiday in Fiji. Superstitious women hoping for relief from chilblains will fill the bishops' bowls with stew.

And if the revolution really took off, the whole of the Catholic clergy might hit the road. Then there would be squabbles over patches. The mendicant mass would need organising. They would gather somewhere central to elect an organising officer. He would require a base to work from. And someone would inevitably mention a sixteen-room residence going cheap in Lancaster.

Nevertheless I can't help admiring Father O'Donoghue. He's 68 years old.

Like solitary sex

The noisy electrician has been going to the gym for six months now. His Achilles tendon went ping last year and he says he goes to the gym to strengthen it. But really he goes there because he's a runty weed. He's had more sand in his face than a Bedouin.

He has often urged me to join him. I have resisted, partly because all my Achilles tendons are in the pink, but mainly because I am not a runty weed. My mother used to boast that I was sturdy. And once a shop assistant told me I was well-built. I was trying on a pair of jeans at the time and they had got stuck at my thighs.

But the electrician is an insistent man and yesterday I joined him. The gym carpark was loud with music. Through a second-floor window I could see the top halves of people doing aerobics. Incredibly some of them seemed to be men. I was impressed by the electrician's speed and strength as he stopped me getting back into my car.

At reception I had to sign a form that said it wouldn't be the gym's fault if I died. I also had to give a list of my goals. When I said I didn't have any goals the receptionist said I had to, so I wrote 'happiness'. She looked at me.

At the bottom of the form was a diagram of the human body for me to circle the places where I had suffered injuries. I found that if I went back far enough I could circle everything except my crotch. Then I remembered a childhood zip and circled the lot.

The gym was crammed with the sort of home-exercise machines you see advertised on television by women with leotards and teeth. But these machines were different from the ones in people's houses in that they were being used.

Some of the machines had little holders on them. I was the only person there not carrying a baby's bottle full of water.

By way of a warm-up the electrician and I rode bicycles to nowhere. A screen on the handlebars told me the calories I had expended and the kilometres I hadn't travelled. It didn't tell me the degree to which the saddle was chafing my thighs. Nor did it need to.

The woman on the next bike was reading a magazine. I leaned across to read about Prince Harry and discovered some good drinking tips.

After ten minutes I was very warmed up. When the electrician asked me how I was feeling I didn't bother to reply. A visual scan revealed that the thigh-chafing quotient was 93 per cent.

The people in the gym fell into two categories. There were those with good bodies and those with less good bodies. Those with good bodies wore dinky little shorts and singlets. Those with less good bodies wore baggy shorts and T-shirts.

Some of the people with good bodies walked around a lot but didn't seem to take much exercise. Those with less good bodies worked hard all the time.

There were several large mirrors whose athletic purpose wasn't immediately apparent. One man with thighs like half-g's and biceps like medicine balls held dumb-bells in front of a mirror. Every ten seconds or so he knelt before his reflection.

Few people spoke. Even fewer smiled. Some stole glances at what others were doing, but most wore looks of anguish or of self-absorption. We gym bunnies look as if we are engaged in solitary sex. Personal trainers were on patrol, distinguishable by their good bodies, rather less good uniforms and enormous sports shoes full of technology.

My arms have always been strong. On the bench press machine the runty electrician did twelve repetitions and then let me have a go. I chose to stop at ten. Then he did twelve more and I did six. I would have done seven but he stopped me, out of concern for a blood vessel in my face. While he carried on I went to reception to borrow a baby's water bottle. The girl asked how I was feeling. 'Rubbery,' I said. 'That's nice,' she said.

We did more arm weights and leg weights and then we worked on our abs. We lay down and sat up. We crunched and we writhed like upturned tortoises. We groaned and we gasped – although the electrician had learnt to do so silently.

After an hour I said I thought I shouldn't overdo it on my

first day. The electrician said he normally did two hours, but he showed me where the sauna was. I proved to be good at the sauna.

On the way out the cheerful girl asked me if I would like to join. I said I would think about it. I have thought about it. I lead a sedentary life and I think I should. I shall write them a cheque just as soon as I can move my arms.

Living with basil

A friend confided that she would find it hard to live without basil.

'Basil?' I said

'Basil,' she said.

'Oh,' I said, 'basil. I thought you meant Basil.'

I explained that I had known four Basils. One was an affable porter with a bottomless fund of war stories. Another was a bored cricket coach and a keen pederast. The other two were cats.

'No,' she said, 'I meant basil. The herb. Have you heard of herbs?'

I was forced to admit that mine had not been a herbal upbringing. Wild thyme may have grown on the local hills but there was no way it was going to find its way into our kitchen. Besides we had three herbs in that kitchen already: salt, pepper and a fierce brown sauce. They catered for all tastes.

She tried to interrupt but she had opened a deep vein of memory and I was not be stopped.

Salt, I told her, came in a plastic thing we called a cellar. Pepper came in an identical plastic thing that we called nothing at all. You could tell them apart by the holes in the top. Salt had one hole through which the stuff flowed freely when you jabbed it with a fork. Pepper had six.

You could also distinguish between them by taste. Salt made food taste salty. Pepper didn't. The pepper of the day was that dried and powdered stuff that looked like dirty dandruff but lacked its flavour.

But the best of all herbs was the fierce brown sauce. If you liked the stuff you put it on everything. One dab of it made all food taste like, well, fierce brown sauce. It sat on the table like a virility test, and was popular with fathers and smokers, which in my youth were the same thing.

She asked if we had no real herbs at all.

'Well,' I said, 'there was parsley but no one ate it. It served mainly to separate trays of meat in a butcher's window, and even that went away when they invented the bright plastic stuff that could sit all day in a blood puddle without wilting.'

To be fair to her I confessed that we did know the names of other herbs – sage, rosemary, simon, garfunkel and so on – but they played no part in Anglo-Saxon cuisine of the baby boomer times. Had I found a herb in my fishfingers I would have removed it with surgical precision.

If my generation thought of herbs at all we associated them with medieval witchcraft or folk music, neither of which appealed, though if pushed I'd prefer the witchcraft.

She said that I was out of touch and that herbs were in.

'Oh,' I said, 'yes, I know that. You've only got to glance at a restaurant menu to see a list as long as your arm of the herbal additions to every dish. And what a difference they make.'

'Really?' she said.

'Yes,' I said, 'really. They halve the size of the meal, double the price and have no effect on the flavour.'

She said that I was just saying that and I admitted that I was. Furthermore I was meaning it. I told her I had little interest in the foodism that seems to have swept the affluent world in the last decade or two and I had no desire to be the next lisping celebrity chef setting lonely female hearts athrob with a pint of olive oil and a loin of pork.

'But herbs are big business,' she said. 'Herbalism has made a comeback. Traditional herbal remedies can be traced back to the Middle Ages.'

I asked her to correct me if was wrong but weren't the Middle Ages a time when most people were dead by the age of 30.

She said nothing.

I said I suspected herbal remedies were popular with well people. Sick people, I said, went straight to the doctor.

'What about St John's wort?' she said.

I said I didn't know he'd had one.

'But herbs are natural,' she said.

'So,' I said, 'is the tsetse fly. And anthrax for that matter. And death.'

I'd gone too far. She made to leave. 'Stay,' I said, and before she could resist I took her tenderly by the hand and drew her from the sofa. The dogs raised their heads in curiosity as I led her, as, it has to be said, I lead few women, into the kitchen. Saying nothing I reached past the sink full of dishes and the dog bowls and the cat food and I drew from the windowsill a pot.

'Basil,' I said.

'But,' she said, and then words let her down.

'I love basil,' I said. 'It smells of summer.'

Or else say nothing

I just love writing,' she said. 'Don't you just love it, Joe?'
'No,' I didn't say, 'love is not the verb I'd use, my chickadee.'

'And if there's one thing we writers need,' she said, 'it's feedback, isn't it?'

'If there's one thing we need,' I didn't say, 'it's feeding. Big and juicy feeding with dripping hunks of meat and roasted vegetables in gravy thick and warm as blood.' But while I didn't say all that I could see what was coming as clearly as the wench roped to the railway tracks can see the looming cow-catcher and hear the rumbling wheels and smell the whiff of fate and her kohl-darkened eyes grow wide as side plates, as soup plates, as an entire dinner set, and she writhes and shrieks and squirms in an orgasm of terror so delicious and so vulnerable that you just know the hero of the day will come galloping out of nowhere and – but where was my hero? I had no hero. I was alone and doomed. This woman's wheels would slice me into rashers. I was done for.

'So I was wondering, Joe, if you would care to', and here she paused, the executioner's axe catching the sun at the moment of stillness at the top of the swing, and she smiled a smile which no doubt she thought of as beguiling and which I did not consider beguiling, 'if you would care to cast an eye over a little something I've written.'

'Why of course,' I didn't say, 'and at the same time would I care to take a pair of knitting needles heated over a bunsen burner to the point of incandescence and slide them slowly up my nostrils before tapping them home with a cabinet-maker's hammer? Would I care to? Oh God.'

'Well,' I said.

'I always read your column, Joe, and I've got one your books, so, well, you know.'

'Oh yes, I know,' I didn't say, 'I know exactly what you mean. I recognise your iron logic, the same logic that decrees that every

45

time I buy a packet of frozen peas I can summon Mr Wattie round to dig my veggie garden. Yes, how reasonable. Yes, of course, right.'

'What sort of writing?' I said.

'Oh Joe,' she said, 'it isn't any *sort* of writing. It's just writing, you know, it just comes as it is, don't you find that? That it flows, and you really don't know where it comes from.'

'No,' I said, 'I don't find that at all. I find it hard.'

'I do think,' she said, 'writing ought to be spontaneous, don't you?'

'Yes, yes, of course,' I didn't say. 'In much the same way as I think the designing of an aircraft carrier should be spontaneous or the building of walls or the ...'

'I think it might amuse you, Joe.'

'All right,' I said, kneeling and sweeping the hair I haven't got to one side and laying my neck upon the block, 'I'll have a look at it.'

'And don't spare me,' she said, 'I want you to be ruthless. Tell me what you honestly think or else say nothing.'

'I'll tell you what I think or else say nothing,' I said and rose to go.

'Oh, can't you read it now,' she said, 'here and now? It wouldn't take a minute.'

I took it home. I take a lot of stuff home. I don't know why.

By which of course I mean I know exactly why. I lack the courage to say no. And besides I know why people write.

Words are common property. They're all we have to wring a little meaning from the world, to get some sort of grasp on what and how and why. We want to say things. We are too much alone. We want to understand and, perhaps even more, to be understood. And so we write. It does us good. It acts as therapy. It is the keeping of a diary. It is an exercise in thought. Momentarily it stills the endless whirling of a random world and pins a bit of it down.

From private to public seems such a tiny and obvious step. The diary is words on paper. The book is words on paper. What's the diff? The diff is, well, I took her writing home and laid it on my desk and shunned it for as long as I could shun it and then

46

late the other night I picked it up and read it and made myself a cup of coffee and read it again. And then I put it in an envelope and posted it back to her.

She rang me up. 'But Joe,' she said, 'you didn't say a thing.'

And I could think of nothing to say but sorry.

The end of the soap

The Reaper's trying to put the wind up me but he's wasting his time. Everywhere I go I hear him sharpening his scythe with a noise like fingernails on a blackboard but I don't give a fig. What he doesn't understand is that I've got unfinished business. I mean to outlive my soap.

In 1992 the first XI at a school where I was teaching went to Australia to get beaten. They needed money to get there so the entrepreneurial daddy of the wicketkeeper bought them, as one does, a containerload of Indonesian soap. It was called GIV and it was the colour of dung. He sent the boys out to sell it by the box load. Each box held 48. I bought three boxes. That's a gross of soap cakes. Today, after nine years, I finished the first box.

The stuff's still as good as the day it was made – which isn't actually that good – but I intend to use it all. Call me mean, call me stubborn, but it's become a quiet obsession, an obsession that should please the dingbats who insist that the secret of life is goal-setting. There's something about the mute durability of this mass of GIV, the patience with which it merely squats in my cupboard and waits, that excites my competitive urge. I've got eighteen more years of GIV in my cupboard and I intend to take them.

But the Reaper insists in offering me warnings. Only today I went to visit an old friend who isn't old but is in hospital. Two days ago at work he developed hot flushes as if he'd just drunk five pints of Guinness in a sauna. Ten minutes later he was in the cardiac unit having a bottle scourer shoved up an artery in his thigh. Apparently a bit of something had dislodged from the wall of something else, jammed up against his ventricles and starved his heart of blood. If he hadn't been in close proximity to a hospitalful of gadgets he'd have been reaped.

As it was he was able to sit cheerfully up in bed while the white-coated ones went at his plumbing. Furthermore, and I envy him this bit, the whole exercise was played out on a wide-screen

TV beside the bed and he was allowed to watch his own innards being painlessly reamed. All that was lacking, he said, were the slo-mos and the beer.

He's now condemned to a life of margarine but is otherwise hunky-dory and no more likely than you or I to suffer a recurrence. Apparently the medicos were just a little miffed during the post-op interrogation of his lifestyle to discover that he didn't smoke, jogged a lot and drank that hideous green milk. It seems the docs still believe in Sunday school notions of death being the wages of sin rather than the wages of living. They are wedded, the darlings, to the principle of cause and effect, which is all very well in the test-tube but a little less than precise in the big wide world of experience.

Anyway I got great vicarious excitement from someone else tap-tapping on death's door. We all know in theory about time's winged chariot but this chap had come nose to nose with its radiator grille. I drove home from the hospital with scythe-sharpening noises ringing in my skull, made a cup of coffee, checked the e-mail and got another dose of the Grim One.

A friend in Germany had written to tell me she'd been flattened by a BMW. It left her prone and all unnoticed on the autobahn with the life dripping out of her. But then who should stroll along but her hairdresser, and he of the combs and curlers did the needful, stemming the blood, summoning the ambulance and insisting on holding her hand all the way to the hospital and then all through the night. She couldn't speak too highly of Herr Dresser. And, like my pal with the ticker, she is going to be fine. At the same time I couldn't help thinking that if my local barber, with his famously bloodstained apron, were to offer me such support when I was close to croaking, I doubt if I'd want to pull through.

So the evidence is clear that the Reaper's on the prowl in my vicinity, but he's whistling into the wind. I am measuring out my life in boxes of GIV and I am confident they'll see me through to indoor bowls and slippers. What's more I'm going to send a cake of GIV to each of my shaken friends. I shall tell them to use it slowly.

The good rhinoceros

Six-thirty on the morning of my 45th birthday and I woke in bed in Birmingham, England with a small but perfectly proportioned hangover. It was soon joined by Lucy.

Lucy is six. She wanted me to finish a story I had begun to tell her the night before, a story about a good rhinoceros. A bad Belgian chicken had captured the good rhinoceros and for reasons which I forget had tethered it by the horn to the side of an erupting volcano during an earthquake. Now Lucy wanted to know how the good rhino escaped. So did I.

I blamed Mark. He was the father of both Lucy and my hangover. Late the night before when I'd been a youthful 44 Mark had taken me to a website called Friends Reunited. In a few keystrokes he brought up a list of 35 boys we had been at school with. It was an extraordinarily rich romp through the daisied fields of yesterday.

Each of the people on the list had written a brief autobiography. It's hard to do a life in three lines. As written they were all much the same: married to Blank, father of blank children, living in Blankshire and working as a blank for Blank Limited. Nevertheless they made compelling reading. Here, 34 years later, was Bawden, the tiny child who had sat in front of me on my first day at secondary school, now unthinkably father of two, though rather more thinkably working for a bank. Here too was his tormentor Sturrock, Sturrock who had the body of a Greek god and the disposition of a Dalek. He could throw a javelin 1000 miles and Bawden almost as far. He now sells real estate.

It took the worst part of a bottle of scotch to catch up on 35 lives, lives that started at the exact same time and place as ours.

On the bulletin board of reminiscence only one teacher got many mentions – the man who taught me English and who made more difference to my mind than any other adult. He made me think and he made me laugh. When I grew up and became a teacher I constantly stole his jokes.

I've written him a few letters over the years, but we hadn't spoken since 1975. That morning, after I had failed to finish the rhino story and Lucy had gone to school, I rang him.

He took forever to come to the phone. His voice was like the dried brown stringy stuff on the outside of a coconut. Did he remember me? 'Remember you?' he said, 'I've still got the scars.' I asked how he was. 'Lousy,' he said. He sounded worse than lousy. I said I'd visit.

At four that afternoon I parked outside the block of flats where he has lived for ever. In the foyer a sickly rubber plant and a faint unpleasant foyer smell. When I stepped out of the lift on the seventh floor he was there in his dressing gown, gaunt, haggard, his skin the colour of the linoleum, his handshake weak, his teeth few and black, his hair mere wisps, his pain obvious, his shuffle along the corridor as slow as erosion.

A little later he told me he was dying, dropping the words into the chat like a grenade. But he didn't want to talk about it. Instead for the next three-quarters of an hour he made me laugh.

His short-term memory was shot but he knew it and he played it for comedy. And he reminisced. He spoke of teachers I had known by nickname – Dizzy, Killer, Nunky, Weasel. He spoke of them as people. Most were dead.

If this teacher had posted his autobiography on the internet site it would have read: 'Taught at one school for 40 years. Never married. Now retired.' And the general statement would have missed the mark by miles. Truth lies in the detail.

When I left he stood with me until the lift came. I stepped in and said goodbye and the doors closed.

In the park opposite his flat, people in anoraks walked dogs in the windy sunshine, fathers in tracksuits played soccer with their children. I turned to look up at the seventh floor. He was standing at the window waving. I waved back. I won't see him again.

I didn't return to Mark's that night so I never finished the rhino story. I doubt that I would have been able to. If little Lucy had insisted I think I would have said that the rhino perished. She would not have found that satisfactory.

'But,' she would have said, 'it was a *good* rhinoceros.' And I would have had to concede that yes, it *was* a good rhinoceros, but that didn't make any difference.

Scatter the dark forces

'Joe, wake up,' said Mike in a voice tinged with panic, 'wake up and look at my bum.'

Mike had barged into my room shortly after dawn. I opened my eyes, closed them, rolled over and groaned.

'No no, Joe,' said Mike, 'you've got to look. I've just been to the loo. I think I've got worms. Christ, you've got to look.'

'Go away,' I said, more or less.

The early-morning drama was typical of Mike. He generated drama. All his life he's generated drama. He taught me much.

This happened 20 years ago when we worked several summers teaching foreign kids. Each night after the kids had gone to bed we would play marathon games of ping-pong. If I was winning Mike would make me laugh. My game would collapse. Next morning I would stumble down to breakfast and find Mike there already, standing on a table and announcing to the kids that he was still the ping-pong king. The kids all loved him and so did I.

In medieval times the civic powers of London, far wiser then than now, would appoint a King of Misrule. For a week or two a year this character would lead society to mayhem. He took his followers to church and made such noise than none could hear the service. He organised festivities in which authorities were mocked and the eternal pyramid of power inverted. The King of Misrule followed in a line of straight descent from that annual bout of Roman anarchy, the Bacchanalia.

And Mike for me was always King of Misrule. He filled a need in me for peril. I yearn for peril and inversion of the normal way of things, to see the tame conventions of a tame society overturned. But I am handicapped by being tame. I fear the consequences of revolt. Mike didn't. He led me places where I did not dare to go alone. He thrilled and frightened me and made me laugh.

Each year we'd take the kiddies to Heathrow to send them home. The first would leave at dawn, the last at dusk. Airports are among the world's most sterile places but Mike would turn Heathrow into theatre. Our games were infantile.

Mike would climb onto a table in a restaurant that overlooked the massive concourse of the terminal and he'd pretend to fish. He mimed the casting of a line into the space below where I would get our 50 kids to stand and point. A crowd of bored travellers with time to kill would stop to watch. Then suddenly I had to run from out the crowd, a finger crooked inside my lip to simulate a hook. I'd battle Mike's imaginary rod, sprinting back and forth across the terminal but being hauled inevitably ever closer, up the stairs and through the crowded restaurant. Mike reeled me in until I stood on tiptoe by the table. Then Mike would take a rolled-up newspaper and strike me on the head. I fell down dead, the crowd would laugh and clap and then we'd run away, because the air police were after us, intent on hauling us to choky for being funny in a public place.

It doesn't seem like much. It meant a lot to me.

Mike's only place of comfort was the edge. He loved to peer over the cliff to giggle at danger. Morally he was indefensible. He stole and lied and cheated and he loved seducing women. They tumbled readily between his sheets, and yet it seemed that he was really happy only when ushering a girlfriend quietly out the back while yet another rat-tat-tatted at the front.

If Mike worried about money he never showed it. He was generous when he had the stuff and cadged it when he didn't. I never minded when he cadged from me.

I've barely seen the bloke in fifteen years. He's stayed alive as people tend to do regardless of the way in which they do it. The risk-takers survive as well, or better, than the cautious. The up strokes and the down strokes on the graph are simply steeper for a man like Mike. The bottom axis indicating time remains the same for all. So now both Mike and I are middle-aged. Tomorrow he arrives to stay at my place. I'm terrified.

But at least he won't have worms. That day when we were young we went together to the quiet village chemist's. Mike waited till the counter at the shop was busy with women in headscarves. 'Excuse me,' Mike announced to the assistant in a voice that would have carried several hundred yards, 'but I've got worms. Thousands of them crawling round my rectum.' The women melted into somewhere else and Mike was happy, having scattered once again the dark forces of decorum.

Marconi or someone

'Wake up and smell the coffee' has become a catch cry of everyone too idle or timid to think for themselves, but in a moment of unusual empathy – one tries not to do empathy but at times it just sweeps in and there's nothing that a natural empath like myself can do about it – I have just seen the aptness of the phrase. I have, in short, just woken up and, well, smelt the coffee.

Nothing remarkable about that of course except it hasn't happened for the worst part of a month because I've been afflicted with some viral delight that has produced tankerloads of phlegm and turned the world into a place of starkly reduced sensory data. Muffled hearing, all food tasting of polystyrene and no sense of smell. But now, this morning, three weeks and four zillion Panadol later, I slide from my pit, activate the coffee machine and find suddenly that I can smell the stuff. Calloo callay oh frabjous day and all that. The world is sapid once more and it's all right, so much all right indeed that I'm feeling venomous, and there's nothing like the renewal of spite, gall and misanthropy to indicate a man's return to wellbeing.

Do they still make children play that dreadful game in which each little brat has to pretend to be some significant historical character in a sinking balloon and to argue that he – i.e. Einstein or whatever – shouldn't be tossed out to save the balloon because if he fell to his death the world would be cruelly deprived? I expect so. So good for teaching the little darlings the prime virtues of puffing their own merits and denigrating others.

Well the game's wasted on children. They know too little. But in middle age it makes more sense and the number of candidates one would like to see tossed from the balloon becomes legion. Of course it's a waste of time. The omelette's made and the eggs are broken, but I can't see that there's much harm in us oldies sitting on the porch in our worm-riddled rocking chairs grinding our gums and indulging in grubby fantasies. And the bloke I'd most like to see tossed from several thousand feet and spattered is whoever it was – Marconi, Edison, I don't know but I do care – who discovered that it was possible to record music.

If music were a rarity rather than an ubiquity I might even like the stuff. It ought to be good. Plenty of people are keen to point out that the word music derives from muse and is, oh dear me, the most direct form of expression available to mankind, like a spigot banged straight into the barrel of emotion, a form of expression unpolluted by the necessity for meaning. And yes, I can see all that.

Time was when life was tough but silent. The medieval village was a quiet place save for the screams of people dying from nasties that science hadn't got round to finding a cure for. But then a few times a year there would be special cause to celebrate or grieve and they'd wheel out the blind fiddler and the pipe blower and the lute strummer, and the peasants would all be seized by the magic of music.

The other day a bloke I know who plays in some sort of bow-tie-and-dinner-jacket orchestra hauled out his viola in his own front room and played a few bars of something mournful and the room was instantly drenched with sobbing. That was good and potent and lovely.

But Marconi, or whoever, put paid to that sort of thing. By making music available everywhere everywhen he destroyed its wonder. Look what he's spawned. Muzak. Unspeakable boutiques. Robbie Williams. The subliminal tinkling on aeroplanes designed to stop you screaming. The stuff they play while you're on the phone to the bank and waiting for Mr Dogbreath to stop scratching his crotch or fondling his secretary. Cloth-eared teenagers who have gathered to make noise because the young like noise, and who are promoted by wrinkled sadsacks whose time has gone but who have learnt how to make money by exploiting sex and what they are pleased to call youth culture, as if that phrase were not by definition an oxymoron. Walkmans.

Imagine all of that gone. In its stead silence. And if you wanted to hear music you would have to go to somewhere where music was played by people who knew how to play it. It would be exactly like coming round from three weeks of viral misery and smelling the coffee. But it won't happen. We've got musical flu.

Permanent, fixed and safe

'I told him he was a fool,' said the journalist
I asked why.

'Because,' said the journalist, 'he threw in a perfectly good job
– pension, promotion, security, the lot – threw it in and cashed
up and ...'

He paused while the waiter arrived with our lunch.

'And what?' I asked.

'And bought a second-hand bookshop. And not even a decent
one. It's tucked up some side street visited only by dogs and old
women.'

'Not much point in asking how he's doing then?'

'No,' said the journalist, 'there isn't', and he snorted, and we
looked down at our plates. Mine held fish, his a steak in a blood
puddle. He pinioned the steak with a fork and sawed at the corner.
I watched the fibres tear and ooze.

It's not a rare dream, I think, to run a second-hand bookshop.
To spend your more boisterous years wringing money from the
world and then to shrink into a quiet street and spend the balance
of days among tall walls of books.

The world is too much with us. Walls of books keep it off.
Books are the world at one remove. They are permanent, fixed
and safe. They can be beautiful but they can't hurt, not really
hurt. The wounds inflicted by reading, the griefs and fears, are
theatrical wounds, are pleasant pain.

To sit all day amid old books, while outside the traffic hisses
through the wet winter, going somewhere, urgent and frantic. To
see the occasional customer, a quiet soul in a drab raincoat who
wanders along the spines of knowledge, cocking his head to catch
the titles, his nature illustrated by the shelves he heads for.

It is not business, or rather it is as close to not being business
as business can be. Most of the authors are dead and so are most
of the books. The authors who are judged to be live currency will
be taken from the shelves within days of coming in, but most

will prove to be groats or guineas, no longer current in the busy spending minds that throng the city. A second-hand bookshop is a graveyard of spent passions, and the proprietor is the sexton.

I often visit such shops and I do so in just the same way as I duck into a church. It is a quiet place, a sanctuary. I like the smell and the peace and I like the books.

Today I bought for $5 the *Selected Poems of Thomas Hardy*. Hardy made plenty of money from his novels but after *Jude the Obscure* he gave up prose and for the last fifteen years of his life wrote only poetry. It was his way of retiring from the busy streets. He left the new book shop in the high street with its bright pile of best sellers and moved, as it were, to the backstreet and the second-hand shop that just gets by.

On the flyleaf of the book I bought, written in cheap blue ballpoint:

> Danny
> Merry Christmas
> Good luck up the Whataroa
> Happy Reading
> Lots of love
> Jackie.

If that doesn't make your spine tingle we have different vertebrae. I would like to know if Danny read Hardy up the Whataroa. For some reason I doubt that he did. I doubt even that he took the book with him. But if he did, and if he sat with it in the evening, alone, looking out over the deserted valley, he might have found these lines:

> William Dewy, Tranter Reuben, Father Ledlow late
>   at plough,
> Robert's kin, and John's, and Ned's,
> And the Squire, and Lady Susan, lie in Mellstock
>   churchyard now.
> And in the churchyard of the poem the voices of
>   the dead speak:
> We've no wish to hear the tidings, how the people's

fortunes shift;
What your daily doings are;
Who are wedded, born, divided; if your lives beat
   slow or swift.

Was there perhaps some similar sense of withdrawal from the
world that drove Danny up the Whataroa, without his Jackie?
And is it perhaps the same urge that drives hermits into caves,
monks into monasteries, and busy businessmen into the isolation
of a shop selling second-hand books?

   The journalist laid down his knife and fork.

   'I went to see the bloke the other day,' he said. 'In his shop.'

   'How was he?' I asked.

   The journalist mopped the blood from his plate with a piece
of bread and popped it in his mouth. 'Happy,' he said.

Sliding to happiness

One man lies on top of another man. Each man is wearing a latex suit that makes him look like Catwoman. The man on top is also wearing aerodynamic booties.

'Those boots will have an impact,' says the commentator.

The event is called the double luge, the luge being a space-age bin-liner. It slides at 120 kilometres an hour and 20,000 people have come to watch it slide. A well-positioned spectator can see 50 metres of track, which means that he catches sight of the luge for approximately no seconds.

One of the lugists is called Stefan and so is the other one. 'They've been called the sliding Stefans,' says the commentator. The commentator's comment occupies one-tenth of the duration of the run which is handy because there's nothing to say about luging and the commentator keeps on saying it. 'They're very good sliders,' he says, then adds, 'and this is a very good slide.' Because I'm watching the highlights the Stefans take the lead. In the highlights it is always the last team that wins, in a time of roughly two hours after you meant to go to bed.

The double luge is won by two Germans who are not called Stefan. When they win they roll onto the ice for multiple orgasms. Then they stand up and howl to the hills like wolves.

This is playtime in the snow. It's called the Winter Olympics and many of the events take longer to name than to happen. The Women's Combined Classical and Freestyle Five-Kilometre Cross-Country Pursuit is followed by the Parallel Giant Slalom Women's Snowboard.

There is even less to say about the PGSWS than there is about the luging. But someone has told the commentator that it's bad if your snowboard chatters. Silence is golden, it seems, and chattering silver.

A Pole races a Frenchwoman. The Pole's board chatters and the commentator tuts. Then the Frenchwoman falls over and loses. After the race the two women try to kiss but their goggles clash.

The equipment is formidable. Most competitors are dressed like futuristic scuba divers. Their goggles are mirrors, their bodies latex and their suffering invisible.

The ice-hockey players wear a stack of truck tyres with a shirt over them. They skate gracefully up and down the ice looking for someone to ram. In the slow motion replays it transpires that there's also a puck.

You know a goal's been scored because everyone stops skating and starts hugging. Their arms go a quarter of the way round.

This is the Olympics for the northern bits of the Northern Hemisphere. The Africans aren't there. The Kiwis pretty well aren't there. The Scandinavians are there by the thousand and taking it terribly seriously.

The biathlon is an event for Arctic hunter-gatherers. They ski across the tundra as fast as they can and then stop to shoot things. The targets ought to be shaped like polar bears.

The disasters are good. The skiers hit the orange safety nets like suddenly flung crabs. The Venezuelan entry for the luge was a large woman who fitted into her spangly catsuit in the same way as your clothes fit into your holiday suitcase. Halfway down the track she parted company with her luge and her dignity. Gravity tossed her around like a killer whale tossing an elephant seal, then she slid down the last few hundred metres like, well, a dead elephant seal in a spangly catsuit. But she wasn't dead which means that I can admit to having enjoyed it.

Skategate erupted and the authorities reached a compromise by minting extra medals. Thus they avoided admitting what everyone has known for years, which is that in every sport requiring judges, the judges cheat. And Eastern European judges have never forgotten the cold war.

In the two-man bob there are two things that the brakeman must do. He must push the kiddicar as fast as he can down the ice for five seconds and then he must jump in. There are also two things he mustn't do. He mustn't raise his head to look up at the crowd of 20,000 cheering Mormons whose breath clouds the frozen air so that they all, rather delightfully, look to be smoking. And under no circumstances must the brakeman touch the brake.

I was delighted to discover that the brakeman for the Kiwi bob was a lad I used to teach English to. I found myself wondering if, with nothing to do for nine-tenths of the run, he passed the time by reciting poetry. Perhaps he muttered a line from Thom Gunn, a line that seems to me to lie close to the heart of sport: 'One's always nearer by not keeping still'.

But I guessed, on balance, that he probably didn't.

Several worsts

The worst of it is that I shall be fined a fat sum of money. No, I lie. The worst of it is, well, let's start at the beginning.

A windy afternoon, fragile sunshine thin as cellophane, chilliness coming off the sea at 40 kph, perfect for keeping the sand-castle-building, shallows-paddling, shell-collecting kiddiwinks off the beach and leaving it free for me and the dogs and the sticks I shall throw them.

Into the car and off to the beach, stopping only to post a letter to a madwoman. Past the sewage ponds we drive where the wind whips up little brown waves, on the crests of which the sunshine splinters. Right at the roundabout, my three-legged dog barking out the window at the smell of the salt, then over the bridge in, would you believe it, Bridge Street, and stopping at the junction with Marine Parade. Look right, look left, look right again along a road as clear as conscience. Only a single ancient woman hunched against the wind with a sad bag of groceries. The littoral is empty and the whole beach will be ours.

Swing right onto the beach road, then drive 200 yards past the blockhouse surf club with its desolate carpark and the conifers all crabbed from the sand-laden winds, and pull over to park in the bay of rough grass, glancing as I do so, oh so properly, in the mirror. Lights. Lights flashing red and blue in the radiator grille of an otherwise unmarked car.

I get out of my car and so does the cop. The dogs are puzzled. I've no idea what I've done wrong and yet already round the base of my neck unwanted bubbles of schoolboy guiltiness, fear of authority and a sense of being in the wrong are going crawlabout as they've not done for years. And a sort of pricking lightness in my arms and palms. And a knowledge that I'm only a couple of words away from blushing. I hate myself for all of it.

He calls me 'sir'. I don't call him anything. Around his belt the usual uninteresting paraphernalia of enforcement. On his feet the regulation heavy soles. I am old enough to have taught him.

He has stopped me, he says, because I was speeding. I want to say he hasn't stopped me. Here was my destination. I had already arrived and safely. But I do not say that. I say, God help me, 'Sorry'.

'Eighty k,' he says, 'in a 50k zone. That's a little bit excessive.'

Mentally I gesture to the carnage I have wrought in my whirlwind passage down that deserted road. I gesture to the absence of strewn bodies, of orphaned children, of stoved-in sides of houses. But I say nothing. I feel simple injustice, that I, who drive like a spinster, who, since I turned 30 and the hormones stopped their roaring, have had a driving licence spotless as a wimple, who hurt nobody and pay my taxes and uphold the laws I don't find inconvenient, am now having my details laboriously recorded in his stage-policeman's flip-top note book.

'We're having a blitz on speed this month,' he says.

The woman with groceries battles past on the pavement, turning her hunch and her headscarf to look at me, pleased to see me caught. Trouble's good to watch.

'A blitz, a blitz on speed, oh that's just dandy. But not on speed like mine. My speed's okay. The speed you want is hoonish speed, the needless growling adolescent speed of nasty low-slung cars with spoiler-things, the speed of boys and men with horrid haircuts who go fast only to go fast, who speed in just the manner that a rooster crows. That's the speed you should be after, not middle-aged speed in a dirty old car on a poker-straight road with nothing to hit.'

Of course I don't say any of that. Instead, and to my deep astonishment, as if I were the sudden victim of ventriloquism, I hear myself say 'Thank you'. My tone of voice reminds me of a schoolboy in some ancient institution who stands after a caning and shakes his assailant's hand.

The cop drives away. I release the dogs, follow to the beach and kick the sand. The monstrous fine will be nasty but it's not what makes me kick. What swings that kick is petulance, a feeble whine of 'that's unfair', a deep conviction that the rules should not apply to me.

And also, more importantly, the glimpse I've just been granted of the schoolboy I had never much admired, extant still within my ageing frame, as craven, base and whining as he ever was. That's the worst of it.

Sorry, Jim

I'm always banging on about teaching as if I knew how to do it but then I get a letter from Jim. I was paid to teach Jim but clearly I taught him nothing.

Jim's worried about money. Well, that slots him neatly in with everyone else on the planet. People who say they don't worry about money are either saints or liars.

Saints are few and unpleasant. We talk wistfully about them when they're dead but when they're not we don't invite them to dinner. All that self-sacrifice and seeing the best in others can get tedious.

Liars, on the other hand, make fine company. They know how to flatter and how to say deliciously spiteful things at dinner parties and how to pretend that they enjoy looking at our holiday snaps. They're rude as weasels behind our backs of course but that doesn't hurt. And liars feign a lack of interest in money because money is dirty.

Like other dirty things money is exciting. When I was young and poor I spent a fortnight up a ladder painting gutters in a heatwave. My pay for that fortnight came in a brown envelope. I went to the lavatory to open it. It held six £20 notes and I kissed them. It felt good.

Show any of us a bar of bullion and we gawp. We thrill to briefcases crammed with wads of notes. If you want to ensure someone's attention tell them precisely what you earn. Honesty about money is like honesty about sex. And just as we do with sex we skirt round money with euphemisms. We talk of funds and allocations and revenue streams.

Some people will tell you with smug little grins that everything is economics. They are wrong, but they are not massively wrong. Money matters. And so people worry about it. The worriers come in two varieties: those who've got money and those who haven't. As someone said a very long time ago, to have money is a fear, not to have it a grief.

Those who have got it tend to be frightened of losing it. In a lovely novel by the lovely Tibor Fischer a ludicrously rich man lives in terror of becoming less ludicrously rich. He won't invest his dosh because investments go wrong, he won't put it in banks because banks go bust, and he won't put it under the mattress because the world seethes with thieves. Desperate for a place to put his money that is sure to endure, he buys a mountain. Thereafter he lives in dread of earthquakes.

Nevertheless having money is hugely preferable to not having it. I have been poor and I hated it. It meant baked beans on toast and no beer. Yet folk wisdom links poverty with virtue. That's typical of folk. Folk songs, folk dances, folk lore, folk museums, folk everything, it's all ghastly. All folk has every brought is beards, sweaters and an entirely bogus nostalgia for life before washing machines. Folk wisdom is what's left in dank corners of the cupboard of superstition after the hard broom of reason has swept through it.

Poverty is virtuous in exactly the same sense as getting measles is virtuous. Religious tracts may urge us to believe that the poor are blessed and the rich wretched, but that never bothers the rich, because they wrote the tracts.

Anyway, my former pupil Jim is neither a saint nor a liar. He's simply poor. He's got as many children as the old woman in the shoe, and he worries about not having the dollars to feed and clothe them and to buy them battery-operated things from Japan to fry their little minds. Jim works hard but the sort of work he does pays poorly.

All of which is no new story, but dear sweet Jim doesn't want to go in for any of the activities that would earn him more money and in consequence he wonders whether he deserves more money. Clearly I never taught him a thing.

The first thing I should have drummed into his innocence is that the commonest fallacy in the glorious world is that money and merit are linked. Money and merit got a divorce in the Garden of Eden. Merit is a moral thing. Money isn't.

The nurse who wipes the bum and comforts the terrified and loves the dying gets thanks and flowers and smiles in a place where smiles are rare. She gets the pleasure of being needed. But she doesn't get much money.

History is littered with efforts to make things fairer. Some have made a little difference. The rest have failed. Of the people I know who deserve to be rich, a few are but most aren't. When it comes to money, Jim, natural justice is an oxymoron. I should have told you.

Tom, Dick and Harriet

Well, you couldn't wish for a better week. Monday morning and a woman rang to tell me I was sexist. I always welcome praise so I made myself a coffee and sat back to bask.

Two sips of Medaglio d'Oro and I found I'd misjudged her tone. My language, she said, disparaged women.

I had two options. One was to simper with apology, ooze contrition and vow to live a blameless life from that day forth, a life of jerseys, yoga and consciousness-raising.

The other was to hear her out in silence, listening to her frenzy generate its own momentum until it reached a level comprehensible only to bats, watching the froth bubble from the speakerpiece of my modishly 1950s bakelite telephonic apparatus, and all the while waiting for the moment of climactic, indignant, interrogative silence into which I would whisper, 'So you fancy me then, darling?'

But I took neither option. Turning my back to the phone so as to display my yellow streak to best effect I just equivocated until she went away. .

But the week had yet to reach its apogee. The following morning a letter invited me to stand for parliament. You can imagine my excitement. Such vistas opened. The image of self as an MP had so much to recommend it, so emphatic, so decisive, so very right, all that leaving-the-world-a-better-place stuff, all that making-a-difference stuff. How I ached at that moment to make a difference, to enhance lives, to foster, on my own, a society in which we would all link hands and advance singing on the roseate horizon of a better tomorrow, united in the South Pacific, little but big, modest but strong, entrepreneurial, indomitable, like one of those anthem-backed advertisements for Rupert Murdoch's Canterbury Crusaders.

List or constituency – well, what could be more obvious? I had to be down on the hustings, whatever they may be, elevated by a soap box to underline my Radox-cleansed intentions, virtuous and upright and willing to suffer the eggs and ruderies of outraged grass roots, all for the cause.

But then again, I reflected, perhaps not. These days, with everyone waist-deep in Nintendo and cappuccini, ensconced in the I'm-all-right-jackiness of affluence, real political debate is dead and buried. Today is far more list, don't you feel, more now, more germane. No mandate, no constituents. Yes, I would be list. And then I could set about doing good.

It would be a breeze. I could manage the clothing, just, and the debating chamber didn't daunt me. The heckling would be straightforward, indeed a pleasure, and I'm sure I could learn the braying and the hear hears.

I'd be good, too, as scything through bureaucracy. After a near-immediate rise to ministerial status - no footling on the backbenches for me – I would stride into my department, scythe in hand and grin on face, and watch the grey ones scuttle, clutching their briefcases, as I pared the red tape to the bone in the name of the people of Aotearoa. Yes, that would be a doddle. Ditto the press conferences, as I handled with an austere and patrician disdain both the snide and the ingratiating enquiries from the monocellular reporters. Yes, I'd be good at all that.

But then there was the language, and with the thought of the language came the first ant of doubt.

I stood before the mirror and tried to say 'community'. I couldn't. I tried it every which way – 'the Jewish community', 'the gay community', 'the community at large', even 'a community of interest' – but I just couldn't make a noise that made sense. I slavered like an imbecile.

So I tried 'targeting', 'policy initiative', 'strategic input'. Nothing but froth. 'Robust fiscal modelling.' No sound emerged but the burble of saliva.

And then the language ant beckoned the rest of the colony. The taking-things-seriously ant, the belonging-to-a-party ant, the believing-in-theory ant. In they all came and ate away at my dream until it crumbled. I reverted to where I started and my sweet community of one. I rediscovered my utter lack of interest in people in the mass, as opposed to my passionate devotion to people whom I know. I swung back, in short, to my love, not for people in general, but for Tom and Dick and Harriet.

Especially, indeed, for good old bloody old Harriet, a woman who espouses no cause, who doesn't give a fig for the imagined slights of sexist language, who doesn't care about or believe in the notion of women or men in general, but who will defend with tooth and vitriol particular men and women that she knows, a woman who laughs and loves, causeless, merry, heartwarming Harriet.

Natch

Take several gallons of water and dump some sodium laureth sulphate into it, along with cocamidopropyl betaine, propylene glycol, butylene glycol, and a liberal slug of ethoxydiglycol. Add other polysyllables to taste and sprinkle with sodium chloride. Mix, heat, stir and cool, then bottle the result. What you've got is a lot of shampoo.

But before you stick it in boxes and pack it off to supermarkets in the hope that the unwashed millions will make you rich by hauling it from the shelves, you first must christen the stuff. And as you dunk it in the font, what name will you intone over its chemical complexity? Exactly. Got it in one. You'll call it 'Naturals'.

And so would I. And so, more importantly, did the nice people at Colgate Palmolive. They called their shampoo Naturals, and I've just bought a bottle of it and read the list of ingredients.

But before the Colgate Palmolive legal team come rumbling over the horizon waving writs, eager to prove in a court of law that all the ingredients of Naturals shampoo are indeed natural, I am happy to admit they may be right. I am willing to believe that somewhere in Thailand – which is where, by the way, they make their shampoo, for reasons of pure philanthropy and without thought to cheap labour – there are limpid pools of ethoxydiglycol to which the antelope come down shyly of an evening to bathe and sip.

I am willing to believe it because nature abounds in chemicals. Indeed nature is chemicals. Even as I am writing this, the ghost of fifth form chemistry has whispered in my innocent ear that sodium chloride is nothing more nor less than table salt, a substance as natural as malice. Quite what salt is doing in shampoo I've no idea, but neither do I care. The stuff seems to clean my hair all right. No, I have no beef with Colgate Palmolive. My beef is with the word natural.

Natural. Everybody loves natural. It seems like the word next door. A pretty thing with vowels in all the right places and well-proportioned consonants, but also a word so deeply wholesome that you would happily hire it to baby-sit.

But you would be wrong. Natural's a slut. It's the loose woman of the lexicon. Take a tour through the backstreets of the dictionary and you won't find a harder-working whore. In the world of advertising there's barely an executive who hasn't made use of little Miss Natural, who hasn't in some dank alley hugged her flexibility to his black and greedy heart.

Advertising executives love to lie with her because natural has become a synonym for good. Natural means grass and trees and sky and sunshine, gentle birds and quivering delicate antelope. But what we seem to have forgotten is that natural also means bubonic plague. Natural means leprosy and scorpions. Natural means death, drought and prunes.

The opposite of natural is unnatural, by which we mean man-made. And herein lies an oddity. We've come to think that man-made stuff is bad stuff. We couldn't be more wrong.

As Thomas Hobbes famously observed, and as I have never tired of repeating, the life of man used to be nasty, brutish and short. What made it so was nature. Today, by and large, our lives are pleasant, civil and long. And what has made them so is man. Nature gave us smallpox. Man wiped it out. Nature gave us tooth decay and man has given us dentists. Dentists are unnatural.

We have not always been foolish enough to believe that nature is purely nice. It was only in the early 19th century that people began to cherish the untouched bits of the world. Drips liked Shelley wrote odes to the west wind while everyone else took shelter from it. Wordsworth went into raptures over daffodils but had less to say about poison ivy. What they both needed was a week in the mountains in nothing but their underpants. And so do we.

Because then perhaps we might see through the nonsense. When we saw shampoo, or a tub of margarine or an underlay of magnets advertised as natural, we would scoff. The word has slept around too much. It has lost all meaning. It has become merely a nice noise.

Quite why this should have happened I can't tell you. I could hypothesise about the myth of Eden. I could speculate on collective guilt or on the ignorance of urban man. But I think I'll just go and rub salt in my hair.

Sallabout

There are vogues in language. A word surfaces from the depths of the dictionary and for a while everyone in public life uses it, and uses it wrongly. Then the word fades from popularity, sinks back into the dictionary and another arises.

Substantive was such a word. Jim Bolger liked 'substantive'. He used it to describe anything he approved of. Toadies all around him took it up. Then, when he went, it went. In came Jenny Shipley, and with her came 'robust'. She used it to mean substantive. The toadies took it up. Now she's gone I think robust is following her. It will be happy in Ashburton.

But the misuse of some words proves more durable and more dangerous. For a month I kept a list of words that got my goat. It grew long and now I've lost it. But I can remember the first two words on that list. The second one was 'issue'.

Issues abound and they don't mean what the dictionary says they should mean. In fact they don't mean much beyond a vague sense of negative feelings that the speaker is frightened to face. 'There are a few issues around the closing of the Hokitika hospital.' In other and more frightening words, the people of Hokitika don't like it. This evasive use of issue has the texture of a used bandage. With any luck it will go the way of substantive. But I am not confident.

Words help us think. It may be possible to think without words but it's not much use. What we can't express we don't remember. Furthermore, if we can't express it we aren't going to influence anyone else or get much done. There's a limit to what can be achieved with grunt and gesture. If there weren't, chimps would run the world.

I'd thought 'it's all about' was dying. Then I heard John Prescott, the deputy prime minister of, God help it, Great Britain. I once wrote nice things about Mr Prescott because he punched a man who threw an egg at him. I take it all back. I was wrong. Recently Mr Prescott came here to sing unconvincing hymns of praise to St Anthony Blair and to do ra-ra with the Labour Party. He made a speech that consisted mainly of 'it's all about'. Having lost my list, I quote from memory: 'It's all about delivering on your promises. It's all about gaining the trust of the electorate. It's all about winning landslide elections such as the one we just had in which a bit over half of a bit over half of the British electorate voted Labour.'

'It's all about', at best, means 'here's something I like'. It's a grammatical variant of substantive. When used in a speech it operates like a premonitory cough, warning the audience of the approach of something platitudinous but clappable. 'It's all about passion,' says the coach of the All Blacks while neglecting to remind them to catch the ball first.

Petty? Of course I'm petty. Petty derives from 'petit' and 'petit' means small and language is made of small bits called words. Words are bricks. You can't build an edifice with bricks that crumble. It won't prove substantive.

Besides, I've barely started to get petty. What about the hugely popular 'these kind of things'? It's perfectly understandable how this illiteracy came about but to understand all is not to forgive all. To say 'these kind' is like saying 'these brick'.

But 'these kind of' is merely illiterate. I object more fiercely to words that deceive. And prime among these is the word that headed my list of goat-getters. It is 'creative'. I hold no hope that creative will die. It is enshrined in our bureaucracy. We have Creative New Zealand.

Creative should mean inventive or imaginative. It should, for example, be used to describe the very clever man who devised the animation system that made the Americas Cup racing not only understandable but even enjoyable. But it isn't. Instead creative is used in a way that makes, as Evelyn Waugh put it in perhaps his most memorable phrase, my bowels shrivel. Creative has been appropriated for the exclusive use of bad artists. Creative describes the people who write, paint, pot or sculpt things that other people don't want to buy. Creative has come to mean corduroy trousers, and misshapen sweaters spun from pure self-indulgence.

If I hadn't lost my list I could go on. But I have so I won't.

Because he is a man

Oh, it's so tedious and wrong. A judge or two has had a peek or two at a dirty picture or two. And so, say some, they shouldn't be judges.

Every male has his own private porn studio. It's called his head. At peak production shortly after puberty it can churn out a dozen reels a day of startlingly original material. It needs no prompt. It gets no encouragement. Indeed it gets the opposite of encouragement. It gets a pasting from every moral pulpit in the land. Each man is taught to hide it. Each man is taught to feel shame. And yet the studio carries on in blithe disregard, pumping out its steaming torrent of images.

It does not corrupt its owner. It is its owner. Man is a lust-racked beast. We can and do pretend this is not true. It is true.

In later life the dream factory becomes less fertile. It still rolls out the films but it cribs more of its ideas from screen and print. And there is and always has been a wealth of material to help it.

We have pornography in Latin and in Greek. We have the Karma Sutra and the nudes that Titian painted to titillate the Pope. Porn is as old as writing, as old, indeed, as drawings on the walls of caves.

Today it is an industry. In the United States the porn industry is bigger than the car industry. The internet is crammed with porn. It is so because men want it. It is not good that it is so. It is simply so.

I may have met a man who has never riffled through a skin mag or watched a blue movie or dwelt on images that stir him, but if I have I don't know who he is. And I do know that I have met thousands, and I am one of them, who have in their time done all of these things. And we are not bad men. We are men.

'All men are rapists,' screamed the strident women some 30 years ago and they were mad. Very few men are rapists. A randy man can also be a kind man. A lusty man can be good. A man can surf the internet for porn and also be a judge, a fine and honest, wise and decent judge.

A judge has a job to do. To say he cannot do that job because he is randy is to talk startling nonsense. It is to say he cannot do the job because he is a man.

Men are capable of self-knowledge. Men are capable of knowing what is good and what is right while still being men. Their lust does not blind them. If it blinded them then all men would indeed be rapists. But we have will and judgment and reason and sympathy. Without will or judgment or reason or sympathy there would be no courts of law, no civil society, things that men through history, men subject to lust, have forged.

Lurking behind all this is the presumption that people in authority should be androids, unstirred by the emotions that beset the rest of us. With this presumption comes a hideous delight in exposing their frailty. We pillory the judges, princes, kings and courtiers for having red blood in their veins, for being just like us. We pelt them with the sour tomatoes of hypocrisy. It is, I think, the least appealing feature of that animal called man.

Women know men are randy. And they want men to be randy. Women strive to attract men. They may pretend otherwise, but behind all diets, all make-up, all pretty clothes, lurks an evolutionary urge to be sexy. But women also want men to be trustworthy and to restrain themselves and not to make unwelcome advances. It is tough for men. Come here, say the women, and keep your distance. It is the endless dance of the mating game. Porn says only come here.

We live in a sex-driven world. Strip clubs litter the land. Increasingly the strippers are male. *Ladies Night* drew huge crowds. Because it happened in the theatre, that bastion of middle-class propriety, countless women went to watch it with an almost easy conscience. Were any of our female judges among them? And if they were, do they differ one jot from their porn-surfing counterparts?

Yes they do, because they attended *Ladies Night* in their own free time, whereas at least one of the male judges surfed for porn while at work. He used the court computer. He committed a crime, in other words, comparable with filching office stationery.

He should be punished as all of us should be punished who have filched office stationery. Let him who is without sin cast the first roll of Sellotape.

A serial preacher

Boy could I preach.

I preached to children. For two years in Canada and three in New Zealand I ran boarding houses for schoolboys. And those boys got preached at. Multiply, serially preached at. I could turn it on like a hose. Give me an occasion, a grief, a theft, a fight and I would summon the children, loosen the tap of language and drench them with preaching. It was a joy.

Time and again I told them that all that mattered in the end was people. That tears spilt over toys or tractors, CDs or cricket bats were idle tears. That trinkets and money and status and cappuccino makers were all just fine and dandy, but that if their faces were ever to crease into the lineaments of uninhibited joy or grief then what would do it was people. Neither the Porsche, nor the fame, nor the bank balance, nor the delirious clapping of the distant crowd could do it. People, I told them, would stretch the amplitude of their lives. I said it time and time again, I who lived alone with dogs. The children sat in silence until I had finished and then they went away.

I preached tolerance. The hobbyhorse was my image. I said each man had a right to ride his hobbyhorse howsoever and wheresoever he wished, and so long as he knocked no one else from his own little private hobbyhorse, then no one else had any right to knock him from his, no right to make him swerve, or steer a different course, or even to think of braking. The boys sat in silence until I had finished telling them of hobbyhorses and then they went away.

And I preached on virtue. I told them that years of experience had taught me that the greatest of virtues is honesty and the second is courage and that I was reasonably confident that the two were the same thing. And I said that the prettiest and rarest of virtues, perhaps a kissing cousin to honesty and courage, was grace under pressure. The boys sat graciously through my sermon until it finished and then they went away.

At one of the schools I taught at there was a chapel, which I was obliged to attend from time to time and always against my will. There it was my turn to be preached at. I sat in silence in the cushioned teacher pews along the back and writhed with graceless impatience to be elsewhere. The sermons were of interest only when they told stories or when they went wrong. When they went right or when they went moral, they went bad. I resented their intrusion. I resented the implication that I needed preaching at. I resented the impotence of sitting and listening. I waited till the service ended and then I went away.

I can remember none of the sermons that I heard but most of the ones that I gave. I could give them now. I thought my preaching differed by being meaty and unpretentious, and the fruit of experience rather than of doctrine. I was wrong wrong wrong. It didn't differ at all, except perhaps in its degree of hypocrisy.

Where did I get them from, these ideas that I preached? I don't know. They were never preached to me, or if they were I wasn't listening. I may, like a magpie, have picked up some pretty bits from books I'd read, or, far more likely, seized on brightly glittering nuggets from that mine of all shallowness *The Oxford Dictionary of Quotations*.

All I know is that I liked to preach. I wanted to impress. I wanted to be seen, or at least to see myself, as a fresh and independent thinker, a bloke who'd been around, a sage of sorts.

I was and am none of these things. Rather I stumbled from day to day, following no moral precepts, choosing always the option that seemed best for me if I could get away with it. When under pressure this preacher curled up in bed and gibbered with distress, sleepless and frightened, hugging a dog for comfort and as far from grace as it is possible to be. And all day long he practised secret intolerance, cursing anyone who rode a hobbyhorse in any way that didn't fit with what he felt was right. And he fretted about money. And lived alone. And scoffed. And knew nothing.

Now I know only that the urge to preach is a curse. And that it's futile. I doubt if any child I preached at ever changed the way he lived one jot because of what I'd said. For that I'm thankful. For the rest I'm sorry. And here ends the lesson.

Eyes right

The button that holds my trousers up came off so I went to the optician.

The trousers in question are my default trousers, in other words the trousers I put on when I don't think about what trousers I am putting on. Made from corduroy the colour of algae they are so moulded to my shape that at night I don't so much take them off as step out of them and leave them standing on the bedroom floor like a pair of Siamese sentries. In the morning I just step back into them and let them walk me to the coffee machine.

I don't blame my tailor for the lost button – I have had nothing but the best from Mr Hallenstein – instead I blame that thief of all things, time. Time has sucked my mighty shoulders south. If he keeps it up, by the year 2030 I'll look like the Pyramid of Cheops.

When I went to sew the button back on I found that time had also shrunk my arms. I could no longer hold a needle and thread far enough away for me to focus. I tried to pass a blur through a blur.

Once or twice I succeeded but I discovered my success only at the precise moment when I was parting my fingers to have another go and a fraction of a millisecond too late I felt the tiny resistance of the thread pulling through the eye of the needle like either a rich man or a camel. On the one occasion I did manage to stop with the needle threaded, requiring me only to seize the short end and pull it through, I seized the long end.

I could of course have used a magnifying glass but a magnifying glass needs holding and I was already holding the thread, the needle and my breath.

Do you know the difference between an optician, a dispensing optician, an optometrist and an ophthalmologist? Nor do I, but they are all like trap-door spiders. The phonebook revealed that there were thousands of them out there, all previously unnoticed by me, waiting with the patience of time itself for the inevitable day that would bring me and my wallet stumbling into their den. I chose the optician who printed his phone number in 36-point type on the grounds that he seemed like a man who knew his market.

There is pleasure in submitting to expertise, in handing your problem over to a man who knows. My optician was charming, patient and ridiculously young. He reassured me that the eye-test wouldn't hurt. I hadn't expected it to hurt. Now I did. But it didn't. He swung lights around, presented me with charts and diagrams, fixed an extraordinary machine in front of my face and peered deep into my eyes in the way that lovers are meant to but in my experience don't unless they're psychotic or dogs.

And having tested all that my eyes could do he popped onto the bridge of my nose a pair of slotted lensless spectacles that looked as though they had been forged by a neolithic blacksmith and into one of the slots he dropped a lens and asked if that was any better and I said it was worse and he said good, and then he dropped another lens in front of it and then another and then another and suddenly all was as clear and bright as the first morning of spring, and in the manner of a man who had just performed a conjuring trick he asked if that was better now and I said yes it was and I was most impressed but I had been hoping for a horn-rimmed pair.

With the aid of a cross-section diagram of an eye, a diagram similar to one that I remembered copying into a school exercise book in the early 1970s and labelling vitreous humour, aqueous humour, retina, iris and Dave Collier's a Prat, he explained that the lens in my eye was ageing. A baby can focus apparently on the tip of its nose – and from my limited acquaintance with babies it seems that most of them do – but gradually the eye stiffens and the focal length extends and forces us ultimately into the optician's lair.

The optician and I agreed that I could probably go a little while longer without glasses but we both knew as we said goodbye that it was really au revoir. He and time have got me on a thread and they can and will soon wind me in.

'Oh and by the way,' he said, as I went to close the door behind me.

'Yes?'

'Pull your trousers up.'

Going with logs

'You think,' said Tim, 'that time is linear.'

'I do?'

'Yes, you do. But it isn't.'

'It isn't?'

'No,' said Tim, 'time's logarithmic. Experience is logarithmic. Life itself is logarithmic.'

'Is it? Are they? I see,' I said. 'Would you like another beer?'

'Yes,' said Tim. And then as I rose with the glasses, 'You do know what a logarithm is, don't you?'

'Oh yes,' I said.

And I do know what a logarithm is. It is, or at least it was when I was at school, a number that came in a grey booklet, a booklet that was as thrilling as a railway timetable for Eastern Europe and made just as much sense.

And I know something else about logarithms. They marked the point in my education where maths stopped being maths.

I was an obnoxiously keen child. I liked school and could do it. I found some subjects more congenial than others, but I met nothing I couldn't grasp if I chose to do the grasping. And up until the fifth form I could do maths.

Questions like 'If you've got eight calculators and I take away three, how many calculators have you got left?' saw me shooting a hand into the air with squeals of 'Ooh sir, me sir, ask me'. Maths was simply numbers dancing and it was immediately evident how they applied to the world I lived in. But then came logs. My little rational mind ran full tilt at logs but crashed and crumpled against their unforgiving walls. I just couldn't understand them.

That was bad and belittling. Worse and more belittling was the inescapable evidence that others could. Dave Collier could. Dave my mate, whom I loved because he was brave and bad, Dave who threw chemicals in chemistry, Dave who brilliantly drove an English teacher to the psychiatric ward, Dave who regularly landed me in life's deeper bowls of soup, Dave understood logs.

I persevered for a bit. I learned to use logs by rote in the same way as a parrot learns to say, 'Good morning Mrs, how's your knickers.' But when they threw in calculus as well, it all became too much for me and I ran.

It was like the moment when a stream on a mountain ridge flows fractionally to the east or the west. That moment dictates everything that follows. So there in the fifth form some people went east with logs and calculus and headed towards the rational world of science and eventual fat salaries. The rest of us went west. We tumbled towards the pretty world of poetry and imprecision and poverty. We would never build bridges but we would write ditties about the grace of their arches, or we would lean over their parapets and think thoughts as moody, black and swirling as the water below.

We would deal with feelings. They would deal with facts. And each party felt superior to the other.

It seems like a fundamental human difference, a distinction as ancient as man. But it isn't. It is a modern notion. Renaissance Europe saw no such distinction. Old Phil Sidney knew all there was to know of contemporary science but still spent his evenings knocking up sonnets.

Only around the end of the 18th century did feeling and thought divide. Sensible chaps like Watt invented steam engines while less sensible chaps like Coleridge wrote *Kubla Khan*. And all, presumably, because Coleridge couldn't do logs.

So when last week in an pub in a ridiculously expensive part of London, Tim the oil-engineer told me that life was logarithmic, I felt a sense of trespass. Science was his field, but life was mine.

I put more beer in front of him and asked him to explain. What he said made sense at the time.

'We are middle-aged,' he said, 'and time is accelerating.'

'It seems to be,' I said.

'It is,' said Tim. 'Less happens to us in a year now than happened in a week at university. And less happened in a week at university than happened in a day when we were seven. And less happened in a day when we were seven than...'

'I get your drift,' I said.

'The point is,' said Tim, 'you could plot it on a graph. It's a perfect logarithmic pattern. Time accelerates logarithmically and experience does the same. In short, life's a log.'

'I see,' I said, and for a moment I did indeed think that I saw. But then I asked the fool's question.

'But what exactly is a logarithm?' I said.

As Tim explained, the pall of incomprehension descended over me just as it had when I was fifteen. And I saw that I still didn't see at all.

He's in a meeting

Whenever I ring a friend at a place of work and I am told that he or she is in a meeting I suspect that I am being lied to. Furthermore I hope that I am being lied to. I would not wish meetings on my friends.

The least nasty kind of meeting is the large-group kind. You can always rely on a loudmouth to hijack such a meeting. This allows everyone else to doodle at the back. The loudmouth wants to ride his hobbyhorse, a matter of great concern to the loudmouth but of none to anyone else. It is the chairman's job to push him off that hobbyhorse. The loudmouth is reluctant to be pushed off and the friction can be fun to watch. When the meeting is adjourned the agenda will be half completed and the loudmouth fully enraged.

A common feature of large-group meetings is the procedure expert. He is always a he and often bearded. He delights in seconding motions, insisting that people speak through the chair, and saying 'Point of order, Madam Chairperson'. He has no other contribution to make.

Large-group meetings become worse when they are divided into small-group meetings. Sometimes an amusingly overpaid facilitator is employed to facilitate this. With great skill he facilitates the gathering into little groups who each have a subject to 'brainstorm'. Brainstorm means to come up with ideas. The vogue for brainstorming stems from the belief that there is no such thing as a dumb idea. As it happens there are millions of dumb ideas. They are deemed worthy of attention only in brainstorming sessions. The group's scribe summarises the dumb ideas with a primary-coloured felt-tip marker on a remarkably large piece of paper.

Then all the little groups are facilitated back together into a large group for what is excitingly known as a plenary session. This is the only extant use of the word plenary. Plenary derives from the Latin plenus meaning full, but plenary sessions are rarely full because during the tea-break several people have snuck off. At the plenary session the scribe for each of the small groups displays the remarkably large piece of paper and speaks to the ideas on it. Meeting experts say 'speaks to the ideas' because only the ideas are listening.

When all the ideas have been spoken to, the facilitator summarises the meeting and sends a security company to collect his fee. Then someone on a lower salary collects all the remarkably large pieces of paper and stores them in a cupboard for future reference. Future reference means finding them five years later and throwing them away.

But most meetings are not large-group meetings. They are small-group meetings called by management. Managers summon their underlings for the purpose of consultation. They wish to stimulate a co-operative and productive workplace environment and to build team spirit. At the start of the meeting the manager briefly expounds his own point of view. When that hour is over the underlings expound their points of view. When that five minutes is over, so is the meeting.

Some people like meetings. They see themselves as ideas people. They go from meeting to meeting sowing ideas in the manner of a mayfly depositing eggs. Others do not see them as ideas people. They see them as people who don't do any work.

The most popular topic for discussion at any meeting is the topic that was discussed and not resolved at the last meeting. It is not resolved at this meeting either. Cue for the second most popular topic of discussion at meetings: the date of the next meeting. This discussion can occupy a remarkably large part of a meeting.

Managers often call meetings to ensure that things are being done. Calling the meeting ensures that, for the duration of the meeting, things stop being done. The people who are attending the meeting know that the things will still have to be done and that the meeting will not affect the way that they are done. It will affect only the amount of time available for getting them done.

In short meetings are rarely good things. They stop work being done, they arrive at predetermined decisions, they create the worst possible atmosphere for the generation of ideas, they cause resentment among the industrious, they are hijacked by fools and they gratify only the vacuous.

So when I ring a friend at work and am told that I cannot speak to him because he is in a meeting, I hope, for the sake of my friend, that I am being lied to. I hope that the only meeting he is attending is with porcelain or coffee. And I suspect I am often right.

I wish they didn't

It's a pity the Americans speak English. It makes it hard to see them as foreign. But foreign they are, as foreign as Turks, as Uzbeks.

It's absurd of course to discuss a quarter of a billion people as if they shared a common character, but at least I won't be hamstrung by facts. I know little.

Two weeks ago in Florida I rented a canoe. The canoe-renter was the authentic Southern thing – pick-up truck, moustache, cat hat and a drawl like dripping treacle. He told me he had always wanted to go to New Zealand. I said he should. He paused by the river to think in the intense gelatinous heat.

'Now would I have to be getting me a passport?'

I said he would.

'That's not a problem,' he said. 'And would I have to be changing my US dollars?'

I said he would.

'That's not a problem.'

He put the canoe into the water and me into the canoe. 'Now you all be having a nice paddle, do you hear me?'

I said I did and I would. And I did. Small alligators, big otters, pileated woodpeckers, snapping turtles, basking turtles, catfish and a spring-fed river as clear as Hemingway's prose. But most of the way down this river out of Eden I was preoccupied with thoughts of the canoe renter. What was it that made him American – for he could not have been anything else? Was it the courtesy, the affability, the insularity?

Years ago I travelled down the West Coast of the States – as far away from this Florida river as Brazil – and I travelled light. I carried only a backpack of prejudices. Cherished prejudices, racial heirlooms that I was unwilling to let go.

I had been raised to see Americans as energetic children, committed to making money and being keen, but all of them, in the words of Evelyn Waugh, who was and who remains my favourite bigot, 'exiles uprooted and doomed to sterility'.

After three weeks of thumbing and catching buses, I knew that either I had been sucked in or Waugh was wrong. These people were different, but if I had to choose a single adjective to describe them I would not choose sterile. I would choose good. These people were good.

The young did not seem disaffected. The old seemed free from bile. Their interest in me was all that I could wish and their generosity was greater than I could handle.

At the small town where I stayed last month in Florida the highest paid member of the university staff is the football coach. Each Saturday in winter 85,000 locals turn out to watch his team. It's a team of kids, 20 years old, too young to drink. Some of them weigh 300 pounds – in metric terms that translates to just over two people.

At game's end, win or lose, they kneel to pray. God's big in the States, almost as big as the breakfasts. I love the pancakes. 'Short stack or tall stack?' they ask. A short stack is a meal for two. A tall stack is a meal for America. They beat the world in fat. They beat the world in bigness. They beat the world.

Paul's Diner was cheap and dark and empty, the pancakes syrup-drenched, the coffee thin but unlimited, the service uniquely courteous. It is an endlessly polite country. By the griddle a little placard. 'Praise the Lord,' it said.

I caught a bus to a shopping mall. The passengers were poor and black. They talked. They did not know each other but they talked. This was no English or New Zealand or French bus. This was more like a bus in India.

A girl nattered to the driver about her wedding. In the gaps in conversation she read at random from a book. The book was called *Prayers that Much Avail*.

I wanted books for the long flight home. In the whole monstrous air-conditioned shopping mall the only books I found were a ceiling-high stack of Bibles, King James version, both Old and New Testaments, nicely printed and a dollar each.

Hanging outside countless houses the stars and stripes. And written in windows and on placards jammed into lawns, the words 'God Bless America'. If anything sums the country up it's that strange slogan – part prayer, part statement. Somehow it lies at the heart of the huge and insular country that leads the world, a country that can relish Disney World, a bewildering engaging dazzle of a country, a country that seems bereft of irony until you watch the brilliance of *The Simpsons*, a country that made all the global running in the century just ended, a country that I know I do not know, a country that I wish did not speak English.

Hitchlie

I used to hitchhike a lot.

That of course is precisely the sort of thing that middle-aged dull dogs say in order to convince themselves and others that there was a time when they were not middle-aged dull dogs. That once they were devil-may-care, that they lived with a whoop and a ha, and a lust for the strange and the dangerous.

The truth of course is dull. I hitched because I didn't have any money. Or because if I did I was too mean to spend it.

But it did me good. Hitching lifts from the sort of people who stop to offer lifts – psychopaths, homoeopaths, and other lovelies – I learned one fine thing. I learned to lie.

Hitching is repetitious. The where-are-you-going chat, the why-are-you-going-there chat, the what-do-you-do-for-a-living-oh-how-terribly-interesting chat. It was that last chat in particular that bored me to the marrow. That's why I started lying.

My head at the time was shaven to the scalp. For the lice. Or rather not for the lice. Direct sunlight terrifies lice. Shave your lousy head and the lice shriek as one and scuttle into the dark and clammy sanctuary of your ears. There your brain eats them. Or the other way round, I can't remember. Perhaps a bit of both.

Anyway, I'd shaved my head and I was wearing a pair of those trousers with a knee at the pocket that have come back into fashion. I used to carry my passport in that pocket to discourage homoeopaths with wandering hands. Until, that is, I absent-mindedly forded a river.

Anyway my head was shaven and my knee-pocketed trousers were military green. So understandably the strange little man who gave me a lift asked me if I was in the army.

I said yes. It was a lie. It was also a fine moment. Grand vistas suddenly opened, revealing an endless realm of possibility. I could be anyone, invent anything. The world was at my feet. It was like coming through the Khyber Pass at dawn and suddenly seeing laid out before me the whole of the Chatnagoor Plain, the tendrils of smoke rising hesitantly from the yak-dung fires, the tiny settlements burnished by the rising sun, the dew on the

Patapata palms winking like a jeweller's window.

'Right,' said the strange little man, 'what regiment?' at which point things got a bit sticky. But there was no going back.

We should all do it. We should lie with vigour about all the dull things. Things like jobs. 'I'm a quantity surveyor,' says the quantity surveyor at the party and everybody yawns. Why? Because that isn't really what he is. It isn't the heart of him.

No one is really a quantity surveyor. Every quantity surveyor surveys quantities only because he has to feed the gaping brood of nestlings that life has saddled him with. At heart he's no more a quantity surveyor than he's a homoeopath. At heart, like all men, he's a swaggerer or a brigand, a blackguard or a saint. One who gallops to the rescue of damsels in distress, or more likely, and more excitingly, one who does the distressing.

All the dull stuff should be lied about, the routine stuff, the everyday stuff, because all that stuff is feeble at best, a safety barrier of conformity behind which we take shelter. Start to lie and the barrier tumbles. The buckles of the straitjacket spring open and the rich winds of freedom tousle your hair. Try it. It's good.

Tell people you're a safari guide or a pimp. Tell them you've had lice. Or even give them a description of some plain in India, inventing place names and the local variety of palm tree. Either they will believe you and catch your imaginative excitement and become happy. Or else they will see through you. And that will make them happy too. Everyone's a winner.

But lie only about the dull things. Be ruthlessly honest about the bright, exciting things, because these are the things we always lie about. Be honest about money. Tell people exactly what you earn. And be honest about sex. Tell them exactly how and how often. It will be as exciting as a lie. Admit that by far the best thing about sex is looking forward to it. Or looking back on it. Tell them about the dissatisfactions of the business itself. Tell them about the noises. They will quiver with delight. They will be purged.

Of course it can all go wrong. Let it. Going wrong is always more exciting than going right. It leads to stories, stories you can lie about later.

And if disaster happens, well, hitch out of town. As I am about to do now, to my homoeopathy class.

Cosh the teacher

M ore and more people,' said the woman on the radio, 'are becoming addicted to gambling. What we need is education in schools.'

Well, the first lesson in the School Cert gambling curriculum is easy to imagine. It would consist of 'don't'. I find it harder to imagine the second one.

But as it happens gambling is already taught in schools. It's called maths. The school I attended even ran an advanced gambling course. It was called the sixth form common room.

There we played poker with huge intensity for tiny stakes. Our chips were copper coins. If silver appeared on the table a crowd gathered to gawp at the high-rollers.

The star of our poker school was a dour little creep whom I shall call Cosh. Cosh, I suspect, had the odds written on the inside of his spectacle frames. There was certainly plenty of room. Before betting he considered, then reconsidered, then slid the coin forward with such gaiety of heart that it scored a groove in the tabletop. He then paused with his finger on the coin to reconsider his reconsideration. If he let go of the coin he did so in the manner of an Old Testament prophet offering his first-born for sacrifice.

If Cosh laid a bet, the wise threw in their hands. That Cosh went home most evenings with a pocket so stuffed with copper that he limped, says nothing for our wisdom and everything about gambling.

I haven't seen Cosh in years but I do know that he went into insurance and I am told he is now rich. I haven't seen Dave Collier in years either but I bet he isn't.

I loved and feared Dave because he made things happen. To paraphrase Clive James on one of his childhood friends, Dave would have a good idea and shortly afterwards you heard the sirens.

When Dave played poker it was like the weather in Patagonia: you never knew what was coming next but it was sure to be extreme. Easily bored, Dave bet on every hand, normally in inverse proportion to the strength of the cards he held. His cunning lay in the word 'normally'. Dave lost a lot but when he won he won big. Once he bluffed Cosh out of several silver coins. It must have felt lovely.

Because of their natures I am confident that neither Dave nor Cosh is now a gambling addict. But statistics suggest that someone I went to school with is. Let's call him Smith. And if Brighton Grammar School had formally taught a course on the dangers of gambling would it have saved Smith? No, it wouldn't, any more than losing money to Cosh did.

Compulsive gambling is ruinous. It devastates families, careers and happiness. But teaching its dangers in school is as futile as most overt moral education. Ninety per cent of moral education happens in the home and it happens when we're young and it goes in through the skin. Next to nothing goes in through the ears. Sermons don't work. They never have and they never will.

The woman on the radio would no doubt argue that what she wanted was not sermons on gambling but information about it. But even if we ignore the fact that children instantly spot the moral fist in the informative glove, what is there to learn about gambling?

In our sixth form common room there was only one lesson to learn and it wasn't a difficult one. It was that Cosh and the odds were the same thing and in the long run you couldn't beat either.

Common sense tells every gambler that the odds are against him. Addicts ignore that common sense. Their reasons for doing so may be diverse, compelling and tragic but when common sense has flown out the window, moral education won't charge to the rescue through the door. Addicts deserve help and compassion and I expect the woman on the radio does far more to help them than I do. But to suggest that school could have saved them is wrong.

Every schoolkid today can draw you a beautiful picture of a cancerous lung. And a fair proportion of them are so skilled that they can colour it in with one hand while lighting a cigarette with the other. Those same children are also infinitely better informed than I was about the dangers of alcohol yet if you believe what you read in the newspaper they are also infuriatingly better supplied with the stuff.

And we've had sex education for several decades now and the remarkable result seems to be a generation far more likely than their parents to contract gonorrhoea and chlamydia and far less likely to be able to spell them.

Déjà drenched

Twice in my life I have had a glass of wine thrown over me. The first was 20 years ago in Canada. I may have deserved it. The second, well, she had the fillings in my teeth buzzing within five minutes of our being introduced. She told me she was not a morning person, which is like saying you don't much care for oxygen.

I realise, of course, that we all feel the lids turn leaden at certain hours of the clock – me, I'm inclined to slide towards Bedfordshire about 3 p.m., especially if lunch has been good, but nevertheless I am confident that if summoned to defend the motherland or whatever in mid-afternoon I'd be up like a flagstaff and waggling the dagger in a state of alertness that none could criticise. Whereas Miss Lovely gave the impression that if war were declared shortly after breakfast she'd be likely to yawn and leave the heroism to everyone else, on the grounds that as a non-morning person she might get confused over the tank controls.

Now it seems to me that over the centuries the philosopher bods have by and large concluded that life's not a stroll on the flat but more of a steeplechase, and that virtue, happiness and all the rest of it come from striving to hurdle such obstacles as the great timekeeper happens to biff in our way. And it further seems to me that the tendency to feel a bit bleary after rolling from the sack is one of the more easily negotiated obstacles and as an excuse for incompetence and other slackery it's risible.

Perhaps it was her remarkably equine teeth, or her cement-mixer laugh or it may have been the liberality of the flunkey with the foil-necked jeroboam, but anyway it wasn't long before I was expanding on this theory with vigour. It was a lunchtime bash and although the noonday bells had yet to chime, Miss Lovely responded to my expansion with an energy that not only had me leaning a little away from her but also rather undermined her morning-person theory.

And then we got on to patriotism. In reply to her probing I told her that I was not myself a patriot, that I was above all that sort of thing intellectually, but that if called on to do my bit against Johnny Foreigner I'd be the first to brandish the swagger stick. She said that was, and I'm quoting, inconsistent, archaic and ovine.

'Inconsistent?' I echoed.

'Inconsistent,' she repeated. How could I claim to be consistent if I decried patriotism but was willing to go to war?

'But I do not claim to be consistent,' I squeaked. 'I revel in inconsistency. To vow allegiance,' I said, 'to a random lump of rock on which one happens to be born is not the act of a reasonable being, but rather the act of an unthinking primitive, a thug, a pack animal, an automaton of instinct.'

'Yes,' she said, and offered me a smile comprising three parts gall to one part cobra venom.

'But,' I added, in the manner of a player of stud poker hauling an ace from what they regrettably call the hole, 'I am not a reasonable being.'

'No,' she said, 'you're not.'

'No indeed,' I said, 'I am an automaton of instinct *and* I am a reasonable being. I am, as Pope so wisely put it, caught on the isthmus of a middle state, a being darkly wise and rudely great. I am both thinker and doer, both rationalist and lover, both intelligence and feral gut. I am, to paraphrase Pope yet further, both the glory of the world and its jest. And so, darling,' I added with a smile as sweet as one of those appalling Turkish desserts whose name begins with b and which can rot the teeth from 30 paces, 'are you.'

'Am I indeed?' she said in a tone as arch as Marble.

'Yes yes, sweetypie, you are. Consistency,' I said, 'is the hobgoblin of the tiny mind. For example, like you, I am intellectually convinced that women have been oppressed by men. Like you, I am intellectually convinced of the case for equal rights for women. Like you, I am intellectually convinced that women can do pretty much everything a man can do, bar a few physiological functions. And like you, I will argue the cause with any man, woman or management consultant. But, I said, and here's the point, none of that intellectual conviction prevents me from laughing at a good fresh sexist joke. And if you were honest you would laugh too.'

'Try me,' she said, taking a sip from her glass of wine. And I did.

Ruling and sucking

There's a philosophy in the air which people are occasionally kind enough to write to me about. To call it a philosophy is to dignify it beyond its deserts, but here it is anyway. The heart of it is winning. Winners rule, losers suck and there's an end to it. According to this sort of thinking there are but two types of people in this world, those who win and those who lose.

Oddly enough this is the only point where I agree. There are indeed only two types of people in this world, those who divide people into two types and those who don't.

But according to the fans of winning, New Zealand is suffering from losers' disease. Other countries aren't. The Australians, for example, aren't and the Americans emphatically aren't. (The Bangladeshis never get a mention.)

The so-called philosophy of winning comes with a set of platitudes. I have been sent a few by a gentleman who is keen to let me know that I am a cynic and a thorough-going bred-in-the-bone loser, none of which I deny. He informs me that losers have excuses whereas winners have programmes, losers see problems whereas winners see answers, and so predictably on. In short he suggests that if we can only think as winners, any difficulty becomes merely a delightful and challenging little hurdle to be blithely leapt over in the happy gallop towards the Plateau of Plenty, while the great mass of losers huddle in the shadow of the first little hurdle and gibber together as perpetual detainees in the Valley of Misery.

A philosophy is a view of things based on understanding, and understanding is based on observation of what is, not what ought to be. So it is not a philosophy that my correspondent is preaching but an attitude. Nevertheless that attitude is seductive. Being a winner sounds so clean and bouncy and promising. It smacks entrancingly of New Year's resolutions.

It is of course nothing new. It has been around for years under a thousand aliases, of which perhaps the best known is the power of positive thinking. In one form or another it is the preaching to be found in a trillion self-help books. That there are not, as a result of a trillion self-help books, a trillion triumphant tycoons strutting between heaven and earth, suggests that there might be some flaws in the thinking.

I have known only one person who has openly espoused the self-help positive thinking attitude. I will not go into details but he has come, I'm afraid, a cropper.

But I know winners and some of them I love. I could drop the name of a good friend here and you would recognise it. He is a man for whom thought and action are all but simultaneous. He charges into projects with irrepressible vigour. Sometimes he trips. More often he soars. He is fazed by neither. He's dynamic and a doer and a household name and a joy to be with.

Another friend, whose name you would not know, is also a winner. He makes things happen. When his house was flooded and painters came in for a fortnight to redecorate it, by the time they had finished he had formed them into a limited company and got them a contract to paint supermarkets in Nigeria. Yet this man, Roger, does not expect others to be as he is. He is the wisest man I know, and the most tolerant.

Some winners appeal less than these two friends. I do not think, for example, that I would love Mr Kerry Packer, for all that he has winner stamped over every inch of his mink pyjamas.

I have also known and loved people whom my correspondent would condemn as losers. Andy has never won. He is a brave and good man, but something squats in him that debars him from conventional success, a sort of longsightedness that's as heavy as misfortune. It has kept him remote and poor, but not, I think, sad.

To use a phrase that's very old and very simple, it takes all sorts to make a world. To divide people into winners and losers is wrong. Every country holds within its population an infinite variety of people, forged in the womb and the cradle, and then steered down their days partly by chance but mainly by character. And that is how it is and I for one am pleased that it is so. And to talk of winning and losing is to turn life into the black and white and false simplicity of war or sport.

Down at the elbow

Are you a bloke? And around this time of the year do you grow gloomy? And do you have any idea why this is? Do you imagine it's the menopause, or poverty, or the end of the rugby season, or inherited male guilt?

Wrong on all counts. But relax. You are not alone. And besides, help is at hand.

For most of the year I am a byword for bonhomie. People remark on it. 'Look at his bonhomie,' they remark. But then late November rolls around and people pass me by on the other side of the road remarking on nothing. For around this time of the year I pack a big fat sad. My demeanour alters from the frontispiece of *The Bumper Book of Merriment* to Act V of *Hamlet* with a double portion of grief. I sink into a Stygian sorrow, inhabiting the Tartarean depths of misery with only a few classical adjectives for company. My baboonish grin lapses into a coat-hanger. Shoulders hunched, tongue spotted, brow liverish, liver brownish, I earn a little miserable bread from posing for the before shots in Viagra ads.

Until today I had not known why this was so. There I sat this morning at my usual table at that greasy little joint the Elbow, moping over a glass of breakfast and thumbing idly through a second-hand copy of the local rag. Then I turned to the advertising feature on page 28 and the world changed. The scales fell from my eyes with a tinkle that turned heads.

'Keep that tinkling down,' bellowed the Elbow's wizened proprietor, 'there's blokes here trying to be miserable.' But I barely heard him. I was transfixed.

To gain a sense of how I felt, imagine Marie Curie first dipping a finger into a test-tube, withdrawing it, licking it, and realising that here at last was radium. Then add the delight of Einstein fooling around with m, idly squaring c on his calculator and suddenly discovering e. And multiply that yet again by the feeling that swept through Rutherford when he brought his tiny cleaver down and saw in front of him, like a neatly halved apple, the split atom. 'Ooh, golly gosh!' exclaimed Rutherford in his excitement, and so, when I saw page 28, did I.

'Men,' announced page 28, 'are difficult to buy for, right?' And suddenly the universal male misery made sense. Up looms the great religious bash of Christmas when the developed world does one-third of its annual retail spending, and we men just aren't up to it. We stick in its festive craw. Right this moment, women intent on adding to the sum of human happiness are scouring the shelves for things to buy us and coming up with nothing. We've already got a whip and a wetsuit and brace of inflatables and we think the world has nothing more to offer. No wonder we feel miserable. No wonder the end of the year sees us knocking back the Prozac. We are Camus's Outsider, Dickens's Scrooge, Notre Dame's Hunchback all in one, excluded from the boundless joys of Yuletide consumption.

But all that's about to end. Never again need we fear the matching tie and handkerchief set, the cordless drill or the herbicidal aftershave. It was all laid out on page 28. The missionaries have landed and brought with them a store devoted to gifts for men. They call it a 'centralised and specialist gift-purchasing solution'.

And they've done their homework. There are, it seems, only six varieties of men, and the store is divided accordingly into sections, one for each of the six. From Action Man – 'fit, healthy, risky, a gym monkey, an adrenalin junkie' – to Style Merchant – 'relaxed, confident, frequent flyer and gadget geek' – they've got us men speared and sprawling on a pin.

Did you think you just watched a lot of rugby? Pick that chin up. You're a King of the Castle – 'armchair sportsman, handyman and happy homebody, K.C. says "chuck it on the barbie" '. Did you picture yourself as a grumpy old sod who likes silence. Think again. You're a Lone Ranger – 'thinker, strategist, L.R. says "hmmmm" '.

Or do you, as I do, see yourself as a being unique unto himself, an embracer of multitudes, contradictory, enigmatic, someone who defies categorisation. Well we can forget it. 'In a League of

His Own' defines us to the last syllable.

So be gone dull care. Christmas is coming and it's time for us men to cheer up and join in. And if you want to know what to buy for the woman in your life, why not a Mills and Boon? Inside its pink covers she'll find just the men she'd like to buy for.

Be luggage

I like to think that I'm as sympathetic as the next chap, but there are limits. And beyond those limits stand rap musicians. Being middle-aged, middle-class and crusty as a pie, I find rap music unspeakable. But this week I have found myself in the unaccustomed position of feeling sorry for a rapster, oozing sympathy, indeed, like a wounded social worker. It can't go on.

I should stress at this point that the rapster I am feeling sorry for is not Mr Eminem. Apparently Mr Eminem is being sued. Some composer has claimed that he wrote the tune for 'Kill You', a sweet little ballad about murdering women, and that Mr Eminem stole it. But I don't think Mr Eminem has much to fear. He has only to play his music in court to be acquitted, not only of stealing a tune, but also of using one.

No, the rap chap I sympathise with is the one who went nuts on the plane. From what I can gather he tipped back 35 duty-free rums, howled, leapt from his seat, upended a stewardess and sexually interfered with a drinks trolley before being overpowered by an excited purser and a posse of socially responsible passengers. Naturally I sympathise with the passengers' desire to rough the lout up, but the odd thing is that I also sympathise with the lout himself. He did precisely what I want to do on aeroplanes.

Forty-five years have taught me that the only proper way to travel is on foot, with one pair of underpants, an insouciant swagger and a knobkerrie for bopping the natives when they get frisky. It's arduous, painful and testing. If you don't fancy any of that you should stay at home and watch *Our World*. But sadly two bicycle repair men from North Carolina put paid to all that.

Orville and Wilbur Wright yearned to fly, if only to part company with the cruel world that had given them their Christian names. And in trying to build a plane they were following an ancient tradition. People have always fantasised about flight. Gods flew, mythical heroes flew, Icarus flew, Superman flew. But man didn't. Then the Wrights did. With their balsa wood and rice paper they made the dream flesh. That's always a mistake.

Sages down the centuries have been careful to stress that dreams are dreams and quite beyond our grasp. They have portrayed life on earth as a business of disappointment and baked beans, with the joy and caviar arriving only post mortem. Now, I have no way of knowing whether the sages are right about the post-mortem bit, but I do know that when people realise their dreams ante mortem, those dreams have a habit of turning to ashes in the mouth. And so it has proved with air travel. It is less than a century since the Wright brothers tinkered, but how the dream's turned bitter.

The horrors begin at the airport. Airports have no geographical location. They stand like pariah dogs beyond the city walls in wasteland that is neither rural nor urban. Bristle carpet, plate glass, a duty-free shop selling kiwifruit cremes, and gin in London-bus-shaped porcelain bottles, an accessory shop full of inflatable neck pillows and matching his and hers tartan overnight bags with little leads so they can be towed like rectilinear dogs, and an indigenous crafts shop selling, oh dear me, indigenous crafts. All of this stuff owes its existence only to airports and air travel. Take it out of your bag when you arrive and you wonder what suspended your judgment.

Airports even discourage walking. Little travelators carry you along the corridors of self-replicating synthetic materials, air-conditioning and muzak. The whole place is designed to work on you like anaesthesia. Because to an airline you are troublesome. They prefer your luggage. It weighs much the same as you do but it doesn't need feeding or heating or to be shown movies.

On board the technological bird you are pampered by people in toy-town uniforms. You are about to travel several thousand miles and they give you a pair of slippers. They feed you, tuck you up, answer your every whim, smile at you, require nothing of you but your passivity. It ought to be lovely but it isn't. Ancestral voices whisper in your ear that something's wrong. You are sitting down but moving. You are crossing oceans but are warm and dry. You are traversing continents but the view from the seat remains unchanged. You have lost control of your destiny. You have been reduced to luggage.

None of us likes to be luggage. In the end we are all of us, even rap musicians, autonomous beings. Hence the rapster's outburst and my unwonted sympathy for him. Though I suppose, on reflection, it is just possible that he was merely loud-mouthed, ill-mannered, boorish, spoilt, conceited, wrong and drunk.

Gliding through Niceville

Well that's another bus missed. There it goes, rattling up Rich Man's Avenue, and everyone on board except me.

I keep missing buses to Richville. I missed the physiotherapy bus. Up it rumbled some 20 years ago, all flexible and rubbery, and I said 'fad'. I was wrong.

I went on to miss the marriage celebrant bus when all I needed was a hat and a smile. I missed the management consultancy bus, despite my love of jargon. I missed the aromatherapy bus, the personal trainer bus, the designer jeans bus, every bus indeed that has carried people to the nicer suburbs.

And now I've missed one of the best and biggest buses in the history of making dosh. I suppose I could still run ahead up the street and leap on board panting, but there's little point. It's packed now, standing room only, and the fares have risen and the profits thinned. I must face the truth that it's gone. I have missed the financial adviser bus, and I am left on the sidewalk of lamentation.

I had all the qualifications for advising financially: a crisp shirt, a genial manner and a face that isn't actively repellent. I couldn't have gone wrong.

What a clever business, financial advising. How I wish I'd thought of it. Your customers are lovely. They all have money. You never see the poor. You never have to chase a debt. You never have to summon the men in leather with baseball bats to call on addresses that smell of baked beans at dawn.

No, you glide through Niceville raking off your 1 per cent and never having to offer a guarantee. No wonder they've proliferated.

As far as I know the financial adviser was a rare bird until the 1980s rolled in with their torrents of wealth, and consumption so conspicuous you could see it from Fiji. Queen Street was awash with lolly and nobody knew what to do with it. Enter the financial adviser, oozing sagacity. The newly rich came flocking.

The crash brought some hairy moments, but financial advising was here to stay.

Since then the business has straightened its tie and polished its nameplate. There are exams you can take, and letters you can put after your name and professional organisations to belong to. But at heart it remains simple.

There is nothing immoral about it. And there's not a lot that's financial about it. To advise financially the first thing you must know is people.

People with money want more money. But people with money are also frightened to lose it. So they are frightened to do anything with it. To the little man the world of money looks like a pool of sharks and he is scared to swim.

If the little man lost his money he would feel sad but more significantly he would feel foolish. He would have to admit that he had invested unwisely, that he had proved gullible, that the sharks had got him.

So the adviser must inspire the little man's confidence. He must take from the little man the terror of making decisions. He must lead him into some degree of risk and he must give him someone to blame if it all goes wrong. But it is only the client that takes the risk. That's the beauty of the business.

The rest is obvious. Does the adviser need to know about derivatives? Hedging? Junk bond leveraging? Not a bit of it. He needs nothing but a chunk of common sense. He needs only to have listened to his gran.

Don't put all your eggs in one basket, said Gran. Diversify your portfolio, says the financial adviser and he means the same thing. There's no such thing as a free lunch, said Gran. Steer clear of the dotcoms, said the good financial adviser. The dotcoms looked so much like a free lunch, there just had to be cyanide in the sandwiches. And finally, money makes money, said Gran, and the adviser knows this is true.

The wealth of the Western world increases. Look at graphs for the last 100 years and they go up. The World Trade Centre falls and the graphs fall with it, but then up they go again, up to where they were and beyond. They climb at a set rate. Put money into secure places and it grows. If you owe money pay it off. If you've got money spread it wide and safely. You won't beat the market, but if you go with the market your money will gradually grow and it will compound and the growth will accelerate and that is financial advising. The financial adviser is someone we employ to embody our own common sense. Plus a crisp shirt and a reassuring manner and a little jargon and 1 per cent. Any honest adviser will tell you so himself. But I missed the bus. I shall go fishing.

So mother was right

When Michael invited me on a fishing trip in the car he had just bought at auction I said I knew where the trip would end. He asked me where that was and I said in tears.

You see, on the day I left home, my mother, as fine an automotive engineer as ever wound back an odometer, clutched me to her bosom and begged me to promise her just one thing.

'Promise me, darling,' she said, 'never to buy a car at auction.'

As she switched me to the other bosom I took the opportunity to ask why not.

'Because,' she said, 'it's buying a pig in a poke.'

And with those words hanging on the air I disengaged myself from the maternal breast, accepted the little pack of sandwiches wrapped in an atlas, cut the apron strings and marched into the arms of destiny. I turned round only once to see my mother holding up her apron with one hand and with the other tearfully deadlocking the door.

But it was 20 years before the truth of my mother's valediction came home to me. Attending an auction in search of something to hoover up a heavy crop of acorns, I found that the only pig on offer came in a poke. But I bought it for a song and headed home still singing. When I strained for an unusually bass note the pig growled. I tore open the poke and found I had been sold a pup. It is true that I have since trained the pup to hunt truffles and have turned the poke into a serviceable henhouse, but the lesson was not lost on me.

Nevertheless Michael is a persuasive man. He assured me that the car he had bought at auction was barely flood-damaged at all and that the real clincher had been the auctioneer's warm-hearted laugh as Michael handed over the cheque. I went.

And what fishing we had. We filled the car with so many fish that it must have felt it was back in the Japanese flood. Perhaps that's why it stopped. It stopped at a point seven hours' walk from civilisation and with no guarantee that when you got there it would be civil. Fortunately Michael knew what to do.

Then, when he'd finished crying, he opened the bonnet and we stared at the engine in the manner of Easter Islanders staring at a Christmas tree.

Astonishingly Michael's cellphone worked. The breakdown people found it hard to disguise their disappointment on learning that we were on an unmarked track in the middle of the bush and therefore ineligible for their free service. But should we wish to meet all costs ourselves they would send out the local King of the Road. They had us over a barrel and we said yes. The King of the Road, they said, would be along in a jiffy.

Stretching back over our barrel we whiled away the jiffy by reading *War and Peace* to each other twice to the tuneful accompaniment of a chilly bin of fish decomposing.

The King of the Road had a big truck and cellphone. He tapped a tappet or two and then in the traditional manner of mechanics the world over he rang another mechanic, held the cellphone over the engine and asked Michael to turn the key.

The man on the far end of the phone diagnosed a missing tow rope, and soon I was up in the cab of the King's truck chewing the fat about hoggets, pigs, pokes and all things rural while Michael bounced over the boulders in our wake.

We had to turn sharply through a gate. The King of the Road enquired whether I'd seen a gate before and if so whether I thought I could hold one open. I think my unhesitating response impressed him and within only a few minutes the truck sailed through. The car didn't. It slewed sideways.

The King of the Road tried once again to haul it through. The car graunched laterally towards the gatepost. Turning a fetching purple, the King emerged from the truck and informed me he was a bad-tempered chap, though he didn't say chap. He confirmed the accuracy of his self analysis by addressing Michael in a manner unheard since the Peasants' Revolt.

But that was as nothing to his manner once he had glanced inside the dead car. In a wonderful volley of vehemence he informed Michael that he was a markedly dozy man, though only the word dozy is verbatim. Whereupon Michael flushed like a lavatory and disengaged the handbrake.

After that everything was jake. The King of the Road and I had a lovely chat in his cab about townie ineptitude to which I contributed several sincere nods. The King then went on to describe in some detail the modest holiday home he was planning to buy with the proceeds of this rescue while I mentally composed a touching little morality play for the stage entitled *So Mother was Right*.

When it rains

The topsoil on these hills is thin. Underneath it lies clay, clay the colour of mustard, or of pus. Winter turns the clay to mud so thick it will suck off a gumboot. Summer bakes it hard as bricks. A spade can do no more than shave it. But not this summer. This summer the clay is washing from the hills.

Water courses down the stems of grasses, collects among leaves and in hollows, then overflows and noses and nudges down the hillside, turning yellow with the clay suspended in it, joining with other trickles to form streamlets, rivulets, every molecule of water obedient to the same implacable forces, forces that divert it, puddle it, haul it off ledges, demanding only that it travels always down towards the eventual sea.

Cutting across the slope of these volcanic hills there's a track where I take the dogs when it rains. When the falling water hits the track the streams flatten to form puddles that merge into minor ponds. The slowing water releases its suspended freight of clay and deposits little fan-like deltas, impossibly smooth, sheened and tawny with the wet. Every delta is a miniature likeness of large-scale geography, like a satellite snapshot of the mouth of the Ganges.

The dogs are away on the hillside happily failing to catch rabbits by ridiculous margins. Beside me a clay delta perhaps half a metre wide, and because it is faultless and gleaming and intriguing – in short, because it is beautiful – I stamp on it. Instantly the water seeps into the bootprint. With the edge of my sole I carve a channel. Water fills it, reaches the end of it, swells, spills and starts the incremental process of depositing a new and even smaller delta, a fan within a fan. I carve again with my boot, cutting a route to a puddle. The tiny surge of water once again mimics the world at large, draining into the puddle exactly as the Tekapo River, say, drains into Lake Benmore, a gush of current that dissipates as it merges with the mass.

I nudge a little heap of gravel into the path of the stream. The water builds behind the heap until it threatens to overwhelm the lip, like a crowd at a football match on old-fashioned terracing, driven forwards by the spectators surging in behind until a crash barrier folds like a pipe cleaner and the people pour down the terraces like water, but screaming.

I extend and reinforce my dam. With raw cold hands I collect pebbles, then larger stones, jigsawing them for the best fit, plugging the gaps with gravel, wads of mud and vegetation. I curve the dam like an elongated horseshoe, until my puddle looks like the Lyttelton inlet above which I am standing.

The dam grows and pleases me, although if someone were to come along the track I would pretend to be doing something else. My hands are numb but I am sweating. And memories are surfacing like fish. The last dam I remember building was 20-something years ago in Scotland where I was beating grouse. A dozen of us were paid to tramp for a fortnight across moors, flushing birds from the heather and driving them towards distant butts where rich people waited with guns.

On the day in question it was raining. We beaters were driven as usual by Landrover into the heart of nowhere and dumped in what looked like Act III of *King Lear* – rain at 45 degrees, a wind that sliced and no gap between earth and sky. We huddled by a stream like wet chickens. My cigarettes were wet.

Then someone idly started to build a dam and we all joined in. We waded and built and plugged and mended with a will, and though we hardly spoke we forgot the cold and wet and we were happy. And when the crackly walkie-talkie summoned us to start our drive, whooping and laughing we smashed the dam to bits.

The dam that I am building now is smaller than the one we built in Scotland, but it so engrosses me that I fail to notice when the dogs come back from the hills. They are standing behind me waiting, may well have been there for some time.

I don't know why it pleases me to dam a stream – perhaps it is similar to what pleases the dogs when they chase rabbits, something, in other words, in the genes, something of instinct, for them the hunt, for me the urge to remodel a bit of the world, to engineer, to bend it to my will – I don't know and I don't care. I like it and that will do. It doesn't matter. I kick the dam to pieces and go home in the rain.

Gueule de bois

I forget what it was exactly – matching tartan luggage perhaps, or designer sunglasses, or aromatherapy stuff, something along those lines anyway, you know the sort of thing – but it was advertised as '100% Lifestyle'. I ordered a dozen. Any day now they'll land on the doorstep and everything will be hunky-dory.

I need a lifestyle, you see, especially on a wet and mournful morning with a hangover like a rough and sullen beast and a kowhai tree that's turning yellow. Nothing unusual about either of those of course, especially the kowhai. All my vegetation turns yellow. I buy it, I plant it, I water it, I mulch it, it turns yellow. Then its leaves fall off and it becomes a stick, all of which is fine by me. Sticks are low maintenance.

The kowhai's low maintenance too, unlike the hangover which requires incessant groaning, but the kowhai breaks the rules. It does the turning-yellow trick every year. There it stands at the end of winter wet and skeletal with last year's seedpods dangling from it like black rags and I'm reaching joyously for my favourite gardening tool which has an agreeably throaty motor and a bicycle chain with teeth, when the kowhai sucks deep into its unimaginable roots and launches its annual routine of self-preservation. Out of nowhere and nothing it extrudes a cornucopia of flowery trumpets the colour of 60s eggcups. I issue a reprieve and the bees go bonkers. All of which proves once again that the essence of good gardening is neglect and threatening behaviour. Neither works on a hangover.

But a hangover's not an objet de lifestyle and nor's a kowhai tree. If it was it would be advertised in the nicer magazines and we'd all have a miniature kowhai squatting between the balsamic vinegar dispenser and the dehumidifier. But lifestyle stuff doesn't grow lovely from neglect. It emerges fully formed from sweatshops in South East Asia at the behest of American companies with Italian names and no capital letters. Lifestyle stuff comes with art-photography of androgynous men with jaws and cheekbones and women who look like sticks but are the opposite of low maintenance.

Nevertheless I'm looking forward to getting my lifestyle. I'm going to live in it. The demands will be many but I shall be equal to them. I shall lounge all day on ergonomic furniture looking jawed and cheekboned in a pair of fawn slacks with a crease down the front you can cut your finger on and I shall cut all my fingers on it and bleed attractively round the chrome-finish cappuccino machine till it looks like one of those tiny desserts surrounded by sauce rings, as served at the sort of restaurants where men wear lilac-coloured shirts with the collar flattened out à la 70s – but without the medallion and the chest hair, shaved chests being so much more 90s.

Only now the 90s have withered like vegetation and no one has the least idea where we're going. One moment's pause for observation, however, and it's perfectly evident that we're going the same place as always: up Pretension Avenue until we hit Realisation Road. Realisation Road is lined with photographs of us trying to have a lifestyle and imagining that other people are imagining we're having a good time. The realisation is stark and sudden as mortality that (a) we weren't having a good time and (b) anyone who thought well of us wasn't the sort of person it's good to be thought well of by.

Fired by this uprush of self-awareness we abjure the urban jungle and head for the country – so, how can I put it, so, well, so utterly authentic, my dear, and belittling and, you know, focusing – and we buy ourselves a secluded little chunk of it. There we build a GE-free gingerbread house with a wetback and a wood-fired range – honestly, it's the absolute heart of the house, I don't know why one ever bothered with electricity – and surround the place with a few of the more placid and picturesque members of the animal kingdom. But then with horror we discover that our little slice of paradise is no longer a sanctuary cradled in the endless swing of the seasons, honest as the sunshine and dismal as the rain, nor is it a constant and healthy reminder of the trivial nature of our self-regarding former lives, oh no, not that any more. It's now a lifestyle block.

So even in what used to be called the country you don't dare to relax because at any moment a photographer called Shelley with the build of a sparrow and a Minolta SLR 3000 with genuine imitation leather straplet may pop round to take angular black and white snaps of you, the lifestyler, lounging enviably and ergonomically amid sticks. With hangover.

Murder your darlings

'Murder your darlings,' advised Sir Arthur Quiller-Couch, but I didn't have to. Meridian Energy murdered mine.

Sir Arthur was writing about writing, an activity that's always kept a herd of charlatans in business. Bookshops abound in books explaining how to write a best-selling novel, most of them written by people who haven't written a best-selling novel. But still they sell to the wistful, like home-exercise gear to the fat and the lonely.

Sir Arthur's advice is sound but he didn't follow it. His wrote prose so purple you could paper a brothel with it. And anyway the idea wasn't his. He cribbed it from Old Doc Johnson. 'Read over your compositions,' wrote the warty dyspeptic doc, 'and wherever you meet with a passage that you think is particularly fine, strike it out.' Wise counsel, but 'Murder your darlings' is neater.

So there I was this afternoon knocking out darlings at a rate of knots, prose so exquisite that it curled my toes, when Meridian Energy pulled the plug. The desk lamp died. The computer screen fizzled up itself in half a second and lay dead. The dishwasher stopped. The bloodshot eye of the answerphone went black. The house, which I would have described as silent, fell silent. The clock on the oven was blank. Time was in abeyance. Only the weak autumn sun kept at it.

I couldn't work. No one could e-mail me. Though the phone on my desk was dead, the one in my bedroom, for reasons I can't even guess at, worked. I rang Meridian and got, to my astonishment, a human voice, a voice belonging to a customer services operative most promisingly called Youarespeakingwith BeckyhowcanIhelpyou. But it transpired after a brief chat that she couldn't. Yes, she said, she was aware there was an outage. I bit my tongue. No, she said, they didn't at this moment in time know the cause of the outage. I bit it harder. No, she said, she couldn't tell me at this moment in time when power would be restored. I tasted the metallic tang of blood.

'Okay?' she said cheerfully.

I felt the weight of futility. 'Okay,' I said, 'in fact just dandy.'

'Thank you,' she said, 'for calling Meridian.'

And that was that. I had been tossed back a couple of centuries, to a world of rushlights and open fires which I didn't have and bed at dusk which I soon would. So I did what I always do when stuck and took the dog out. Stopping at a café en route for a flat white necessity, I met a sad woman fleeing, like me, a powerless home. She told me she had been doing her accounts on computer when suddenly all the numbers disappeared. She asked what I had been doing. I said I had been breathing life into darlings, darlings that made my toes curl, but I don't think she was listening.

I left her mourning her figures into a short black and went up the hill with coffee and dog to sit for a bit on a rock with thoughts, then back down again to the silent house and a strange sense of impotence.

I couldn't type; I couldn't cook the bacon sandwiches I'd planned for dinner. I had perhaps two hours of fading light, 800 words to write and a body to feed. And the world seemed simpler. That is all. The chickens out the back still strutted, and the dog curled undisturbed by the gas fire that, by a magnificent piece of design, won't work without electricity. The house seemed to exhale and relax. Fewer things could intrude on me. The news I didn't need to know would be less able to reach me. The tinsel of the internet, the endless blurting of the e-mail, the phone calls asking me if I cared to address the ladies' social club could not get through. The hush was deep and ancient. The world is too much with us, wrote lumbering Wordsworth 200 years ago. He could not have guessed what the 21st century would bring, how it would stretch out so many tentacles to wrap around our lives and squeeze the silence out of them. I sat and read and then as the light thickened I put aside the book and simply sat.

Fizz and wallop. Lights came on. The dishwasher reignited. The phone rang. I made coffee and booted the computer into life. The screen was blank. Meridian had murdered my darlings. Gone, all gone. I hadn't even heard them scream. I bet that never happened to Sir Arthur Quiller-Couch. The livid green letters of the oven-clock were blinking HELP.

Seven minutes to live

If you had seven minutes to live, how would you fill them? Would you make peace with your maker, perhaps, or just make a cup of tea and look at the sky, or even make love – though that would leave the problem of the other six minutes? Me, I'd make mayonnaise.

Delia Smith, the celebrated cook, makes mayonnaise in seven minutes flat. She's timed herself, she says, with a stopwatch. Well, everyone finds their own way of wringing pleasure from the world.

The supermarket shelves abound in ersatz mayonnaise, relying for their sales on Hollywood endorsements or an advertising budget equal to the GDP of Poland. But supermarket mayonnaise resembles the authentic stuff as I resemble Paul Newman.

Authentic mayonnaise has the consistency of shaving cream. It blobs, and each blob rises to a tip that slumps. The taste, however, is harder to define, indeed all taste is tough to do in words as the wine wallahs found out long ago. They tell us that a chardonnay has hints of passionfruit, but ask them to describe the taste of passionfruit and they'll be mute. The only certain thing is that it doesn't taste like wine.

The other week I was told by a frank and knowledgeable master of plonk that the tongue in not a very discriminating instrument. It can distinguish only between sweet and sour, and salt and whatever is the opposite of salt (which apparently isn't pepper). He said that all other tasting is done by the sense of smell, which is why when you are ravaged by a cold all food tastes of phlegm.

The taste of mayonnaise is especially elusive. It's as subtle as good flattery. At its best it tastes exquisitely of nothing. It's self-effacing, drawing attention to the brasher foods it complements. The nearest I can come to it are words from Katherine Mansfield on a similar foodstuff. 'Jose and Laura were licking their fingers,' wrote Mansfield in *The Garden Party*, 'with that absorbed inward look that only comes from whipped cream.'

This week I bought some flakes of that crabstick stuff that's fashioned from reconstituted bits of fish then decorated with a reddish tinge and given an authentic-sounding Japanese name, and when I brought it home and laid it on the kitchen bench I thought I heard a noise. I bent down close and caught the crabstick crying out for mayonnaise.

I knew that mayonnaise had eggs in it but that was all I knew. I hauled Delia from the shelves. It was nice to find a recipe requiring things I didn't have to go and buy. Eggs I had in abundance, plus oil and salt and pepper. Delia also called for mustard powder but that was clearly dispensable because (a) no mayonnaise I've met has tasted of mustard, (b) the quantity required was minute and (c) I didn't have any.

Delia told me first to separate an egg. I'd seen chefs do that on television. Television eggs, of course, are different – chefs crack them one-handed and never have to fish for errant bits of shell – but I took my egg and cracked it and slid the yolk from half shell to half shell until the white fell away to a brace of dogs who stood below with jaws agape like giant furry nestlings. My isolated yolk was the colour of that middle traffic light whose purpose I have never understood.

Then, said Delia, holding the electric beater in one hand and the bottle of oil in the other, add a single drop of oil and beat it in. I did as I was bid, holding the bowl still with the third hand that Delia had forgotten. Then another drop of oil, and another and another, beating all the while like an old-fashioned schoolmaster. To my surprise, and just as Delia said it would, the mixture suddenly thickened and resembled mayonnaise. And at that point, said Delia, I'd passed the time of danger and could add a slug of oil. I added a slug of oil. The mixture turned to sludge.

Not to worry, said Delia. Feed the dogs another egg white, and add the sludge to the new yolk drop by drop until it thickens again. I did as bid and watched it thicken, then added a slug of oil.

For the next egg I had to go out to the henhouse, but by now I had learnt caution. Slugs were out and dribbles in. In time I had a bowl of three-egg mayonnaise as rich as Mr Getty, and the crabstick sandwich that it featured in was, as they say, to die for. And had I had seven minutes to live I would have died for it about an hour before I ate it.

Diggers and dozers

Today I sought help from a man who loves what I hate.

I knew him first as a third former, his hands hidden up the sleeves of the jacket he was to grow into. Back then he called me, as was proper, sir.

I remember he built a contraption with two chutes for a fair at the school where he was a pupil and I a teacher. He sat at the top of the chutes with a bucket of eggs. He would roll eggs down each chute simultaneously. A punter who had paid a dollar stood below. And if the punter caught the eggs above his head he won a prize and if he missed he suffered. A crowd gathered and the dollars piled up. I was impressed by the ingenuity of the boy.

A year or two later I taught him English, or at least I issued him with books. He said, as was proper, thank you sir, but as I read bits from the books and made much of the sweetness of the prose or the clarity of the thought or the whatever of the whatever he said hmm. He was always courteous and when I asked for essays he fought words on to the paper but all the while it was evident he was elsewhere. He wanted to be doing.

That's what classrooms are for, of course, to yoke the young together by the force of adult law and let them lick at other ways of being to see how they might taste. And then, when all's been done that can be done to let them know the world is various, they burst the bonds that held them there and go the way they choose. And if the way they choose is honest to the way they are they have a chance of happiness.

Today the boy who rolled the eggs is happy. He runs his own contracting company. He's got diggers and dozers and dirty boots. He makes decisions on the run, deals in tons of substrate, lorry loads of crusher dust and twirling tankers of concrete. Show him a piece of land and he can see the subdivision lurking there and he can make it happen. He likes the thrill of altering and building. He likes the challenge of the dealing doing world. I prefer books.

I rang him today because I'd like a house that backs against the bush but remains within rolling distance of the pub and people. I think I may have found the piece of land to build it on and can almost see the Hansel and Gretel cottage I would like with space for dogs to run and chickens to scratch and far from any neighbours, for neighbours are like going back to school.

I called the contractor because I didn't know what to do next. I can read the relevant documents, can ring the people who can do the sort of stuff I need but I'm an innocent who shrinks from such affairs. I feel like a goldfish in a tank of sharks. I like to read and write and laugh but when it comes to building I'm a third former who knows he'll never grow into his jacket.

And so I rang him up and though he was busy doing this and that – a pipeline here, a new road there – somehow he found time to come round in the sort of truck I don't know how to drive and we went to the place where I would like to live. We got out of the truck and looked at the land with utterly different eyes and minds. I saw a semi-rural dream of silence. He saw gradients and sewage lines and where the slope would need retaining walls. But we both said it was nice.

He said what it would cost to build a road and where would be the place to build a bench, whatever that may be, and how a bit of cash could work particular wonders and what the local council would be likely to require and he made the whole thing seem not only possible but even straightforward. I gawped, still daunted, but also impressed in a way I doubt he ever was in my classroom.

Why it should be that what repels one man attracts another, why the gap between natures should sometimes be so wide that we can only gesture across it, I can't tell you. But I can tell you that I am glad that it is so, and I can also tell you two things that can span that gap: the undervalued virtue of courtesy and the greatly valued stuff called cash. I offered the man cash for his time. He wouldn't hear of it. And so instead I gave him, as in days gone by, a book. And he said, as was proper, thank you, Joe.

He was a pretty good dog

Around midnight last night I went up the hill with my dogs, one of them walking beside me unusually subdued, the other one in a bag over my shoulder, dead. I carried a spade. I knew the spot where I wanted to bury him. Nothing special about it, but some distance from the path so that the grave would not be disturbed.

The hill is steep. The dogs and I have climbed it perhaps a thousand times. I usually stop at a couple of places to pant, and three-legged Abel would always stop beside me, panting too.

He was a big dog, 30 kilos or so, more than half a hundredweight. The straps of the bag bit into my right shoulder and I walked in a slewed hunch, climbing perhaps 20 yards at a time and then pausing for breath. But I didn't unsling him from my shoulder. It would have seemed disloyal.

When I came home at 9 o'clock last night he was waiting for me. He whined with pleasure as I got out of the car. I could hear his tail thumping the deck. But when I opened the gate he didn't come to me. I went to him and he was on his haunches. He tried to get up but his one back leg buckled and he sat down again. I put my hand to the leg and he nuzzled at the hand to keep it away from the point of pain.

I went inside. As I knew he would, he dragged himself to the space under my desk that was his den. For obvious ancestral reasons dogs take comfort from a den. My other dog joined him and I lay on the floor and stroked the pair of them together and whispered to them. Then I rang the vet.

On the phone the vet said he thought it would be a problem with a disc that he could fix with cortisone. I doubted it but I didn't say so. I lay with the dogs until the vet arrived.

When Abel heard the car he sat up and barked. The vet examined the leg and tapped the knee with a little rubber hammer and then drove back to his surgery to fetch the drugs that kill. While we waited Abel licked my face a lot.

I rang a friend who looks after the dogs when I'm away and told her what was happening. She arrived before the vet returned and from the floor Abel greeted her with glee.

The vet sedated him with an injection in the scruff of the neck. A quarter of an hour later when the dog's head had sunk onto his paws and his eyelids drooped, the vet tied a tourniquet around the knee of the right front leg, shaved a little fur from the shin, found a vein and inserted the needle. The dog looked at the needle with drowsy curiosity. I said I would like to take over from there.

There was a little blood in the barrel of the syringe, swirling slowly in the bright blue barbiturates. I pressed the plunger and my dog slumped immediately onto his side. I stroked his ears and the top of his head and his flanks and the band of darker fur that ran from his muzzle and up between his eyes. I asked if he was dead and the vet checked the eyes and gums. The pupils had dilated and the gums turned purple.

It took half an hour or so to lug him up the hill. January 31st was a warm night, with a butter-yellow almost full moon, and by the time I started digging, my shirt was soaked with sweat. At the place I had chosen to bury him the topsoil was only 6 inches deep. My spade rang against rock. I tried a few yards to either side but it was the same.

I picked him up again, still in the bag with his head lolling lifelike from the opening, and I went over the ridge and dug again. At the third attempt I found deep enough soil and I dug for a long time down into the clay.

His tongue was sticking out so I opened his jaws and eased the tongue back. Then I lifted him from the bag and kissed him and laid him as gently as I could in the hole, folding his legs so that he looked all right. His eyes were open. I closed them and they opened again. I sprinkled earth over his body and then over his face, and then because I didn't like to use the spade I scooped the rest of the earth in with my hands. I trod the grave down softly, then sat and looked out over the harbour and the dark hills and smoked a cigarette. The sweat cooling on my shirt made me shiver. Then I went down the hill with one dog.